HEBBURN

HISTORY TOUR

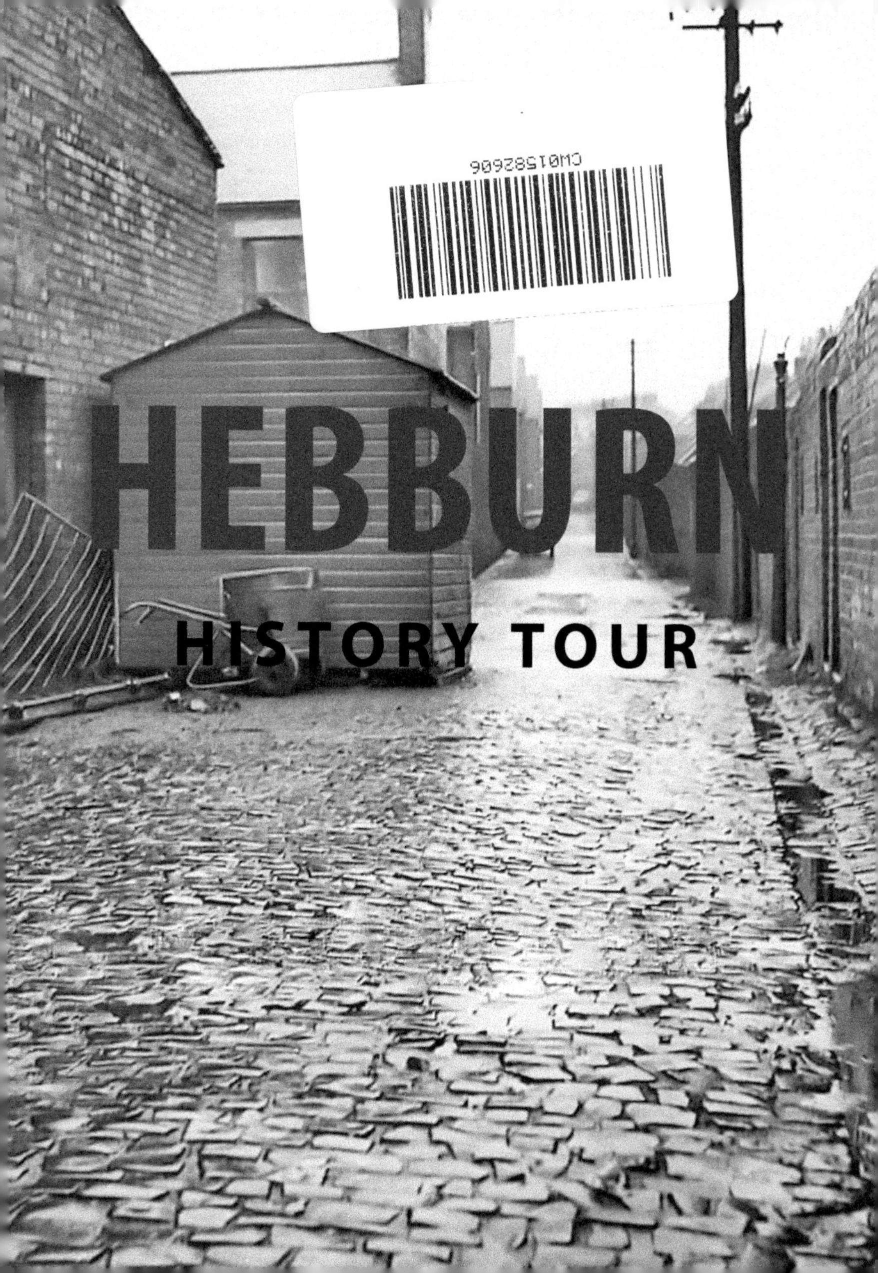

Map contains Ordnance Survey data © Crown Copyright and datatbase right [2015]

First published 2009
This edition published 2015

Amberley Publishing
The Hill, Stroud,
Gloucestershire, GL5 4EP
www.amberley-books.com

ISBN 978 1 4456 5444 7 (print)
ISBN 978 1 4456 5445 4 (ebook)

British Library Cataloguing in Publication Data.
A catalogue record for this book is available from the British Library.

Typesetting by Amberley Publishing.
Printed in Great Britain.

INTRODUCTION

Hebburn-on-Tyne has been transformed since its origins in Anglo-Saxon times. From a tiny eighth-century fishing hamlet it has grown into a modern town covering approximately three square miles with a population of around 20,000. Until the Dissolution of the Monasteries, much of this riverside area was in ecclesiastical hands, but in the mid-seventeenth century the ambitious Ellison family began to make their local mark. Robert Ellison, a wealthy Newcastle merchant, acquired Hebburn Manor, and by 1800 – having been enlarged – this dominated the surrounding landscape.

By 1786, Hebburn Quay was an established 'ballast shore', and six years later large-scale mining operations commenced just to the south-east of the quay, from the first of a series of pits that went on to produce high-quality coal for over a century. Terraced squares of cottages were built near the pithead in the colliery district, and when shipbuilder Andrew Leslie arrived at Hebburn Quay from Aberdeen in 1853 the town's pace of expansion quickened considerably. Although the quay was formerly used for minor repairs to vessels, Leslie was soon recruiting men from Scotland and Ireland to keep pace with orders for his blossoming enterprise, and workers' houses were erected on the riverbank that led to his new shipyard.

Hebburn greatly benefited from rapid economic growth on Victorian Tyneside. Eager to repeat Leslie's success, other manufacturers were attracted to Hebburn, establishing brick, metal and small chemical works in an increasingly busy quayside area. They were joined by the much larger operations of Tennant's alkali works and the Tharsis Sulphur & Copper Co., both of which attracted labour to Hebburn from across the British Isles. Hebburn Newtown had begun to take shape and in 1894 the three districts of the maturing township were recognised as an independent urban district, with Scotsman Thomas Braid appointed as the first council chairman. During this period much of what was once described to 'stand sweetly in the plain' was disappearing beneath the familiar grid pattern of Hebburn's streets, schools and churches.

Of course, like most of its Tyneside neighbours, Hebburn was not immune to frequent economic slumps. On visiting Hebburn in the depths of the 1930s depression, writer J. B. Priestley was appalled by the unemployment and poverty on view. Yet he also commented on the spirited efforts of Hebburn townspeople to encourage self-help and improvement. Near-full employment was established during the Second World War, and post-war prosperity brought slum clearance and renewed expansion to the town. Hebburn's appearance was changing once more. Its confidence was expressed by the creation of a new civic centre in 1967. But further blows were dealt by a subsequent decline of industry and the steady loss of prominent local businesses.

Nevertheless, even in today's new age of austerity, the town has attempted to progress. While they can never provide enough jobs, light industrial and commercial units have replaced many dimly remembered streets. As may hopefully be appreciated from the photographic journey that follows, Hebburn is a small town with a big history. Its people should take pride in their past and have hope for their future.

ACKNOWLEDGEMENTS

Norman Dunn and Kevin Blair contributed much to this compilation. Both provided invaluable information and photographs, and Norman allowed me to reproduce images from his 'Old Hebburn, Jarrow and South Shields' website. This features the work of local photographers, too numerous to name here, but all of whom I gratefully acknowledge. I am indebted also to John Diamond, whose painstaking 'Hebburn Records' are an indispensible reference source and to John Hayton, whose postcard of Ellison Hall started the project off. Other important contributors were Arthur and Thelma Pattison, Jessie Mogie and Alec McDonald (members of Jarrow and Hebburn Local History Society), Ron French, Alan Wright of the Reyrolle Heritage Trust, Colin Mountford, Tony Robinson and the local studies staff at Newcastle and South Shields Libraries. Many thanks also to June and Andrew Dodds and finally to all Hebburn people, past and present, to whom this book really belongs.

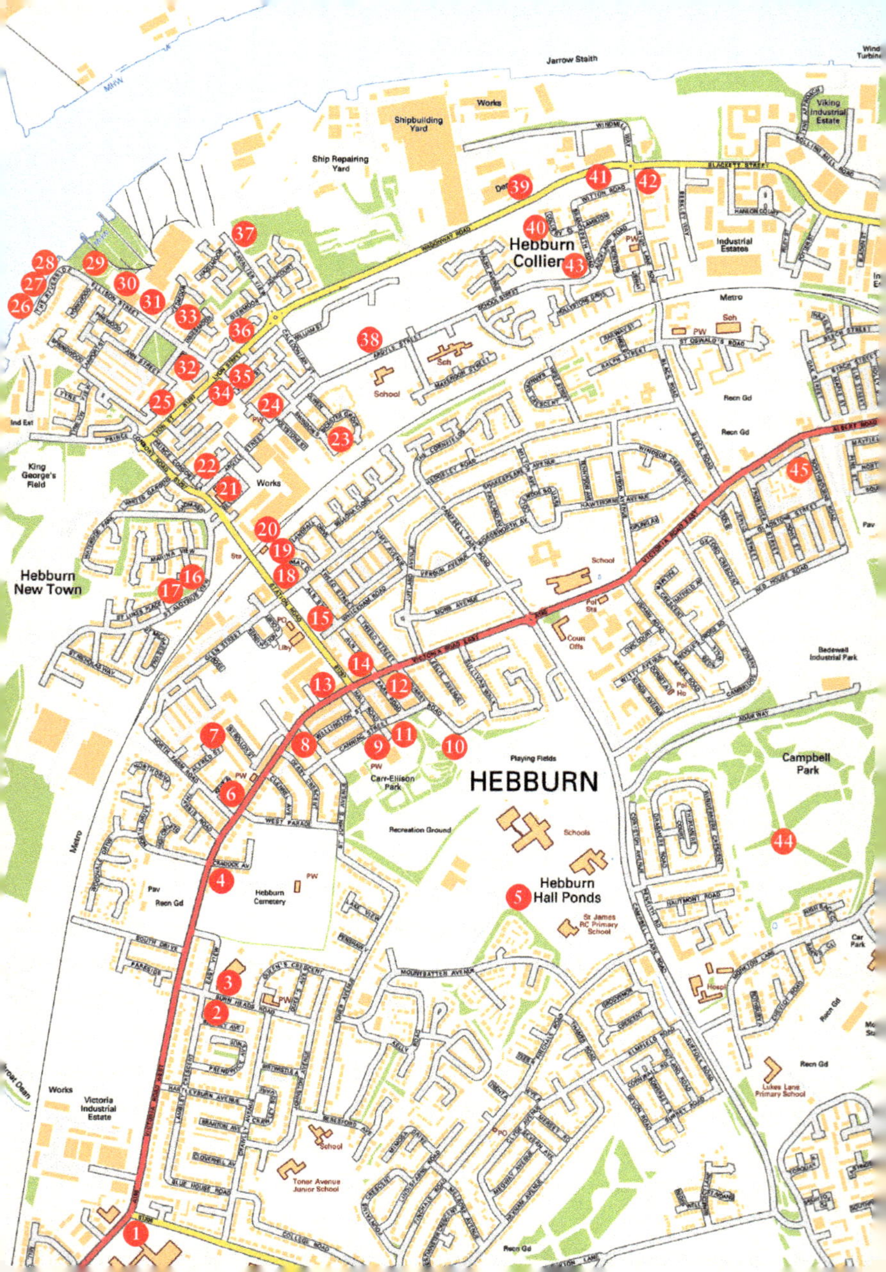
HEBBURN
Hebburn New Town
Hebburn Colliery
Hebburn Hall Ponds
Campbell Park
Shipbuilding Yard
Ship Repairing Yard
Jarrow Staith
Works
King George's Field
Viking Industrial Estate
Industrial Estates
Bedewell Industrial Park
Victoria Industrial Estate
Carr-Ellison Park
Recreation Ground
Playing Fields
Hebburn Cemetery
Toner Avenue Junior School
St James RC Primary School
Lukes Lane Primary School
Metro

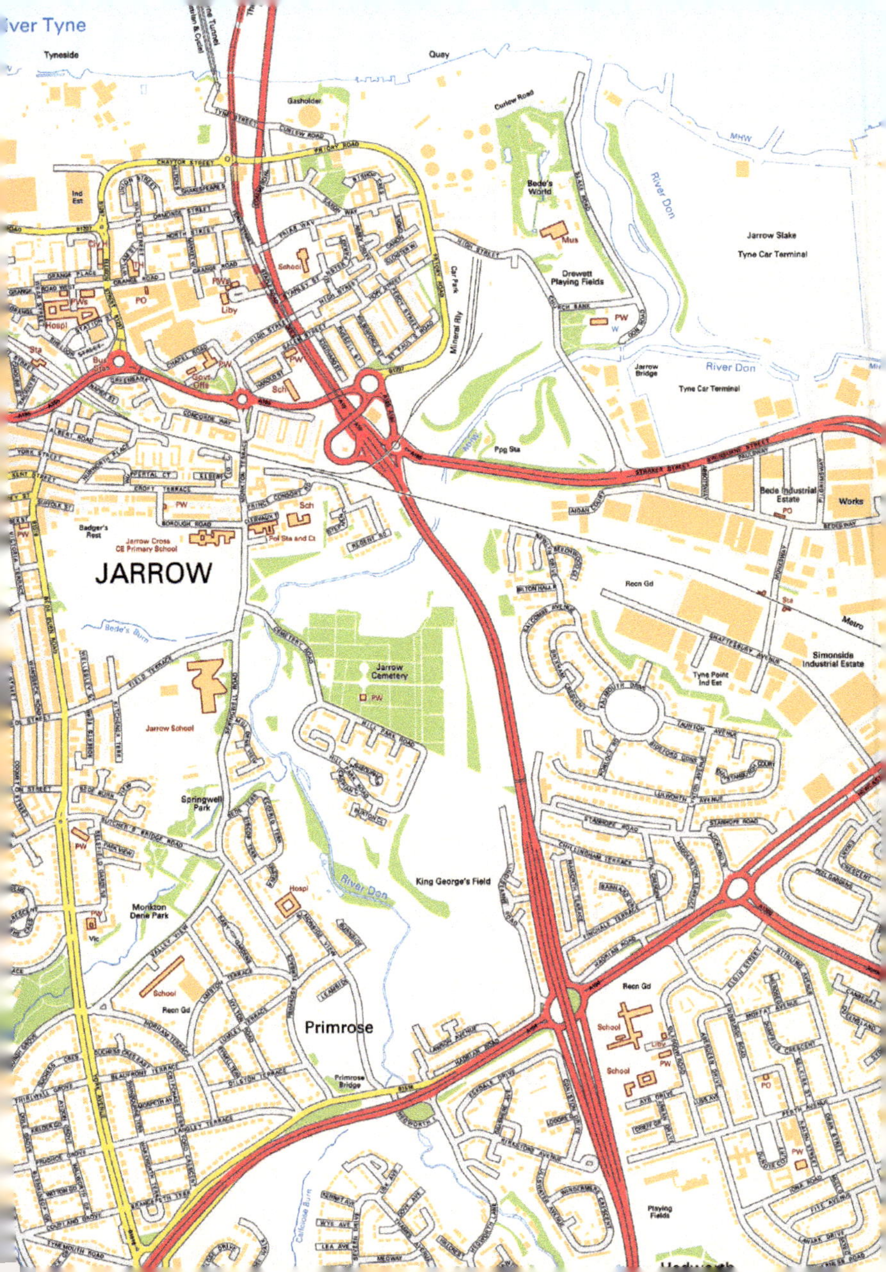
River Tyne
Tyneside
Quay
Gasholder
Curlew Road
Bede's World
Mus
Drewett Playing Fields
River Don
Jarrow Slake
Tyne Car Terminal
Ind Est
School
Liby
PO
Hospl
Govt Offs
Sch
Mineral Rly
Car Park
Jarrow Bridge
Ppg Sta
Bede Industrial Estate
Works
Badger's Rest
Jarrow Cross CE Primary School
Pol Sta and Ct
JARROW
Recn Gd
Metro
Bede's Burn
Jarrow Cemetery
Simonside Industrial Estate
Tyne Point Ind Est
Jarrow School
Springwell Park
King George's Field
Monkton Dene Park
Primrose
Primrose Bridge
Calfclose Burn
Playing Fields

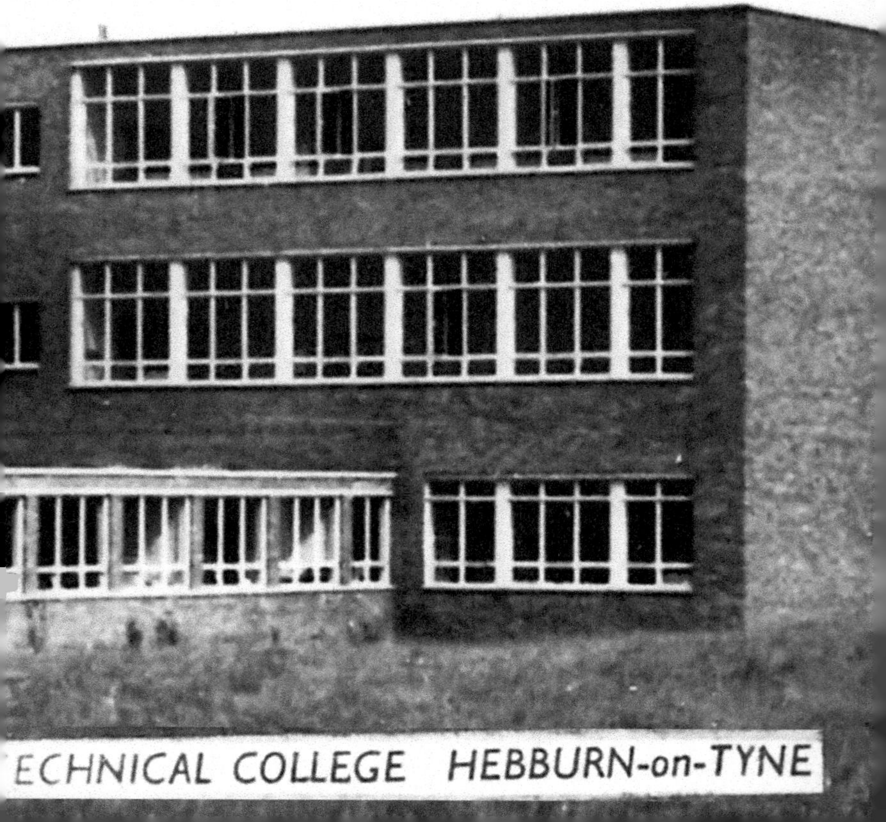

ECHNICAL COLLEGE HEBBURN-on-TYNE

1. TECHNICAL COLLEGE, MILL LANE, *c.* 1957

Hebburn Technical College was opened in 1956, providing further education geared mainly to the needs of local industry. Courses in engineering and mining were on offer and many local apprentices learned their basic craft and technical skills in the 'Tech's' classrooms and workshops. The college amalgamated with South Tyneside College in 1984, but fell victim to education cutbacks and was demolished in 2015. It was built opposite a former reservoir on what was known as Waterworks Road.

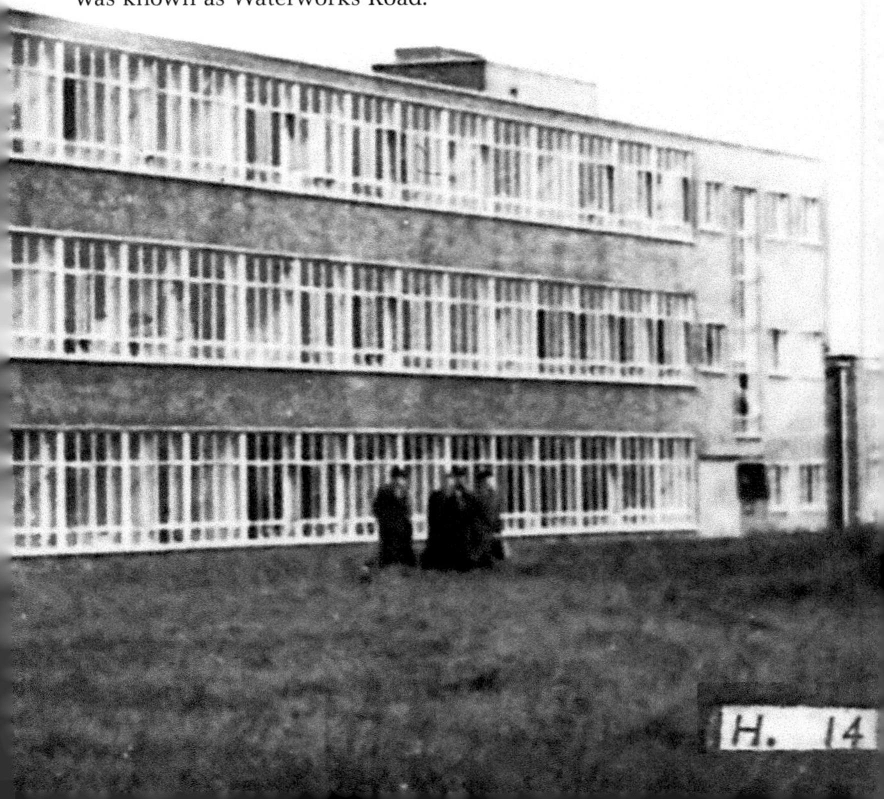

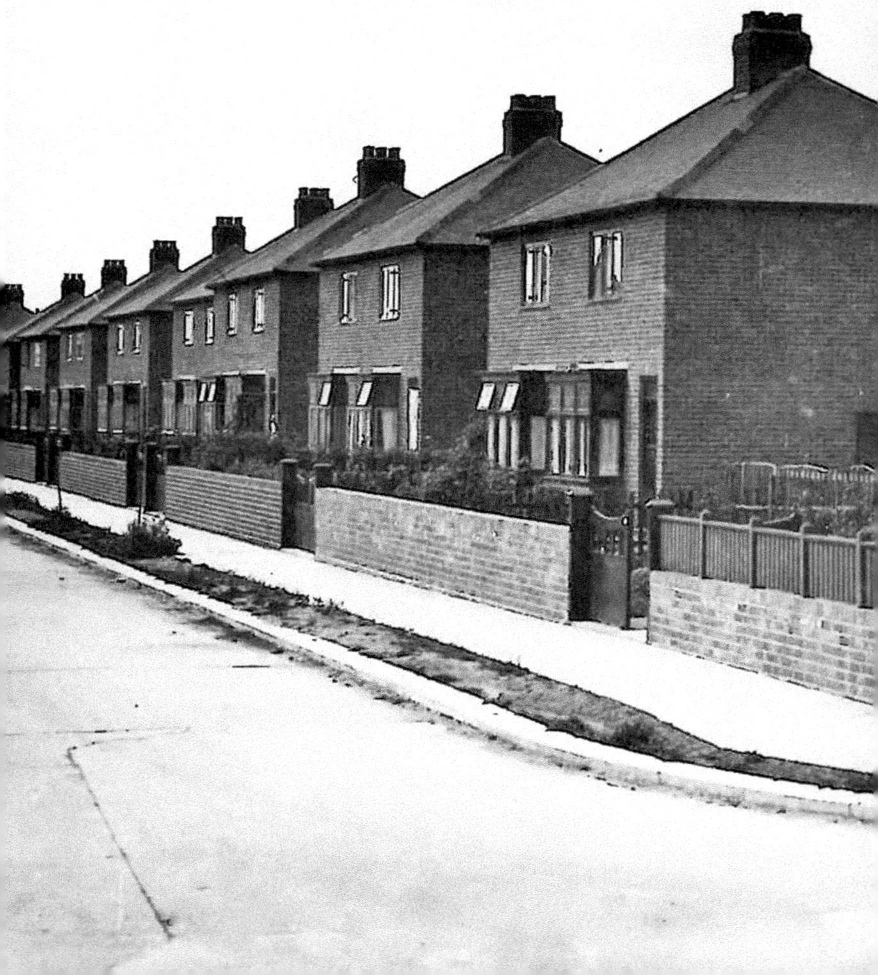

2. LAMBLEY CRESCENT, *c.* 1938

Hebburn expanded during the 1930s despite the prevailing economic gloom. New houses to the west of the town centre on the Reservoir Estate were offered for sale in 1938. They were tucked away behind the main road and within easy reach of Reyrolle, rapidly becoming the town's main employer. Smart semi-villas like these in Lambley Crescent could be purchased from builders J. M. Black for £435 or bought on mortgage for 14*s* 8*d* per week.

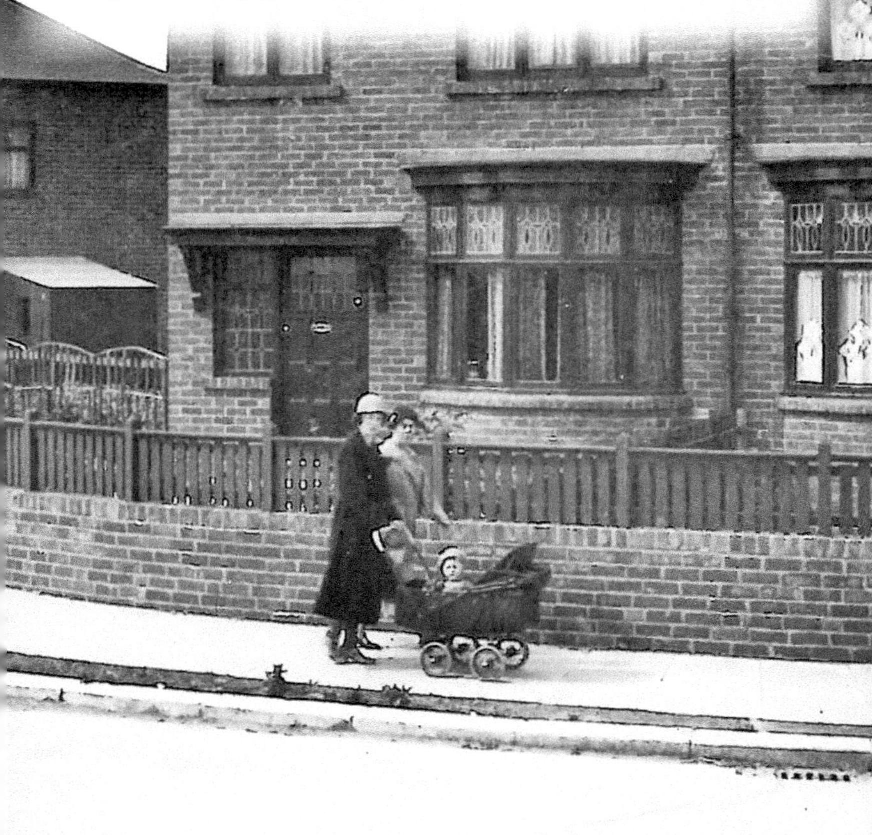

3. OLD 'FEVER HOSPITAL', EAST VIEW, *c.* 1970

Isolation hospitals were a major weapon in the fight against infectious disease. Hebburn's own fever hospital was opened on the edge of the expanding town in 1899, replacing a smaller temporary construction. It was later enlarged to treat smallpox until the 1940s and TB until 1956 when it was dedicated to the care of the chronically ill. Afterwards it became a geriatric unit and is now used as a specialist centre by the NHS.

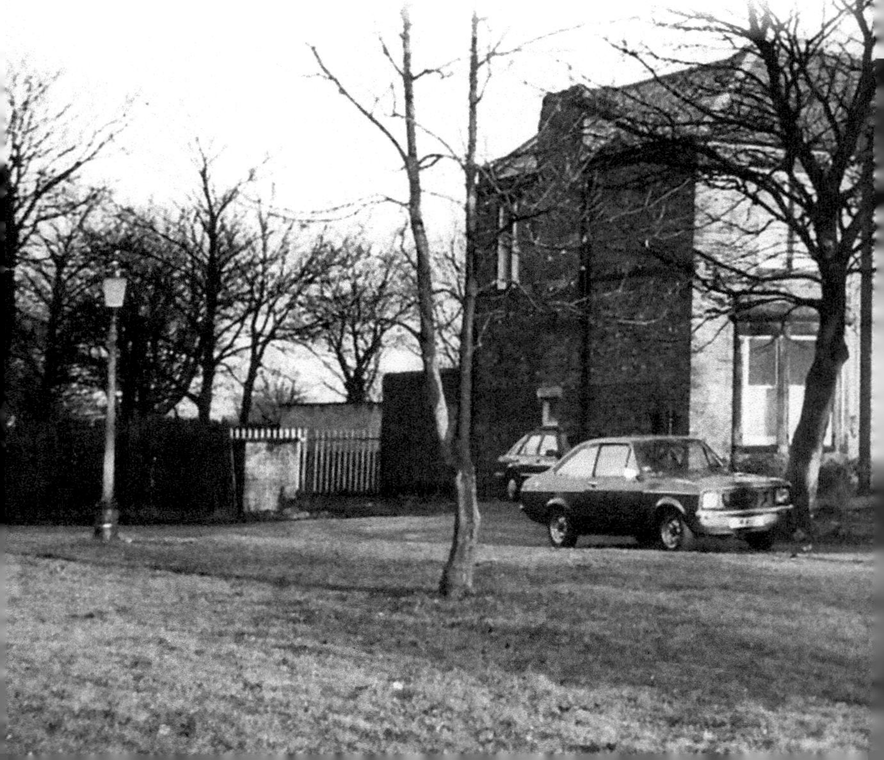

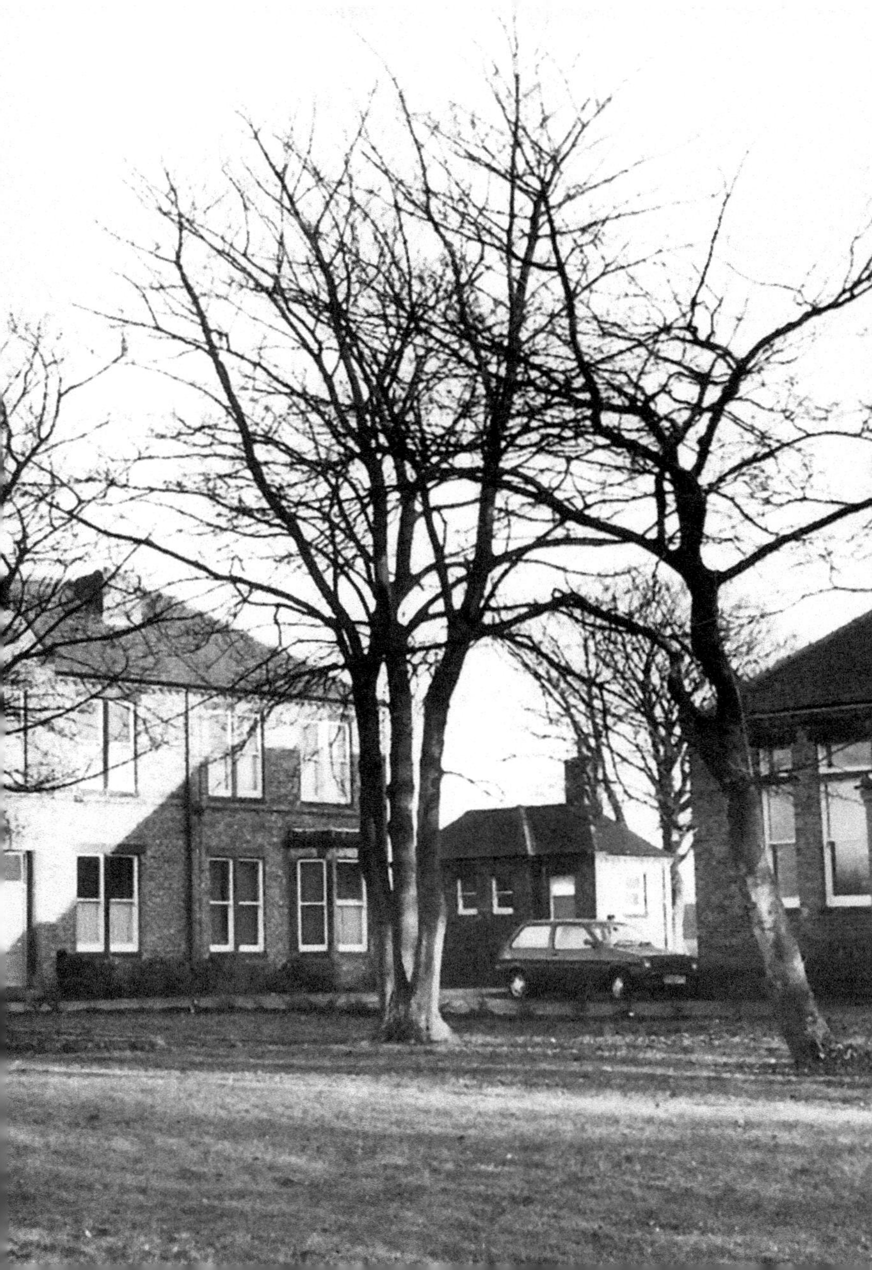

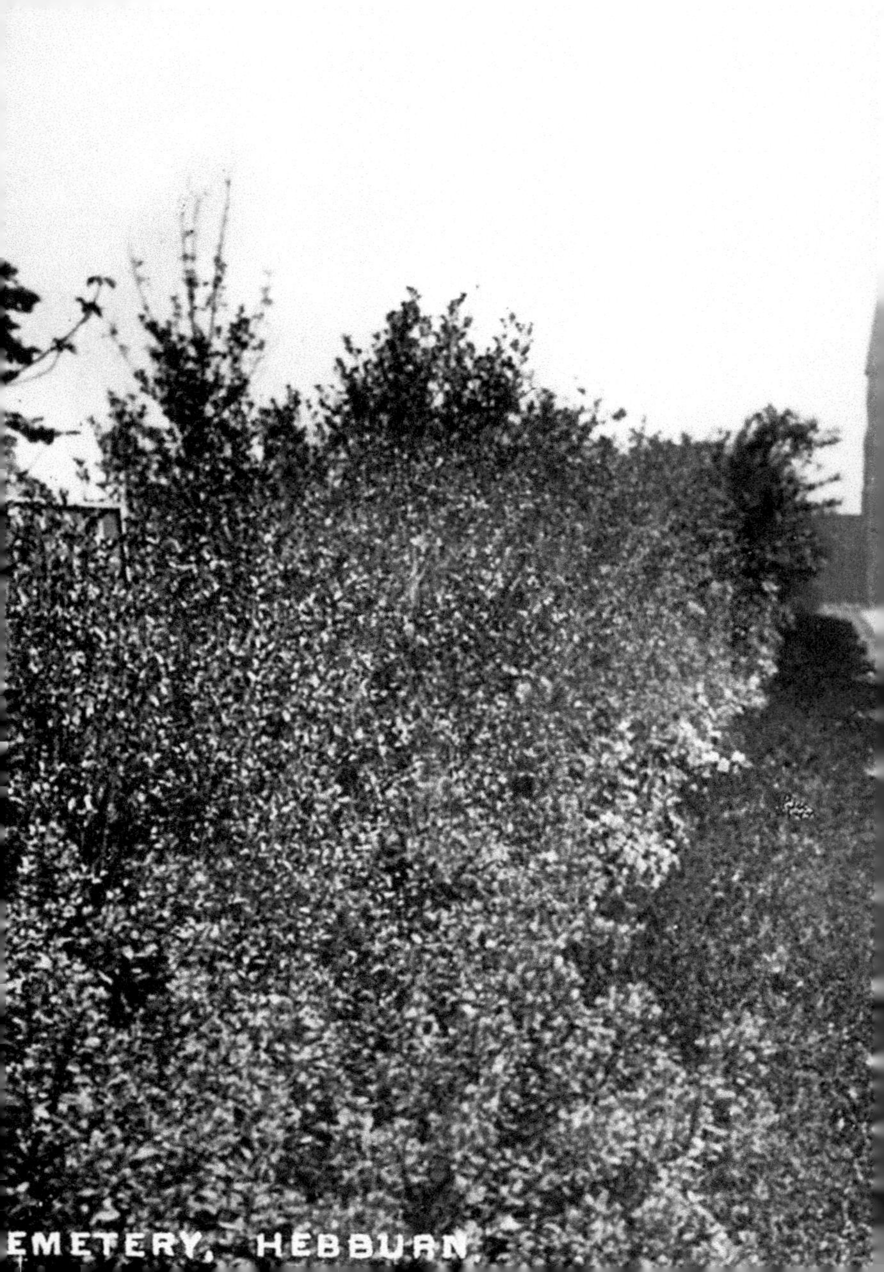
EMETERY, HEBBURN

4. HEBBURN CEMETERY, *c.* 1905

Prior to the opening of Hebburn Cemetery, many local burials were carried out at Jarrow. Bishop Westgate of Durham consecrated Hebburn's new cemetery in June 1890, set out in nine acres of land acquired by the Hedworth, Monkton & Jarrow Burial Board. The long main driveway led to a pair of mortuary chapels, the north originally Nonconformist and the south Church of England, with an arched carriage gateway between them.

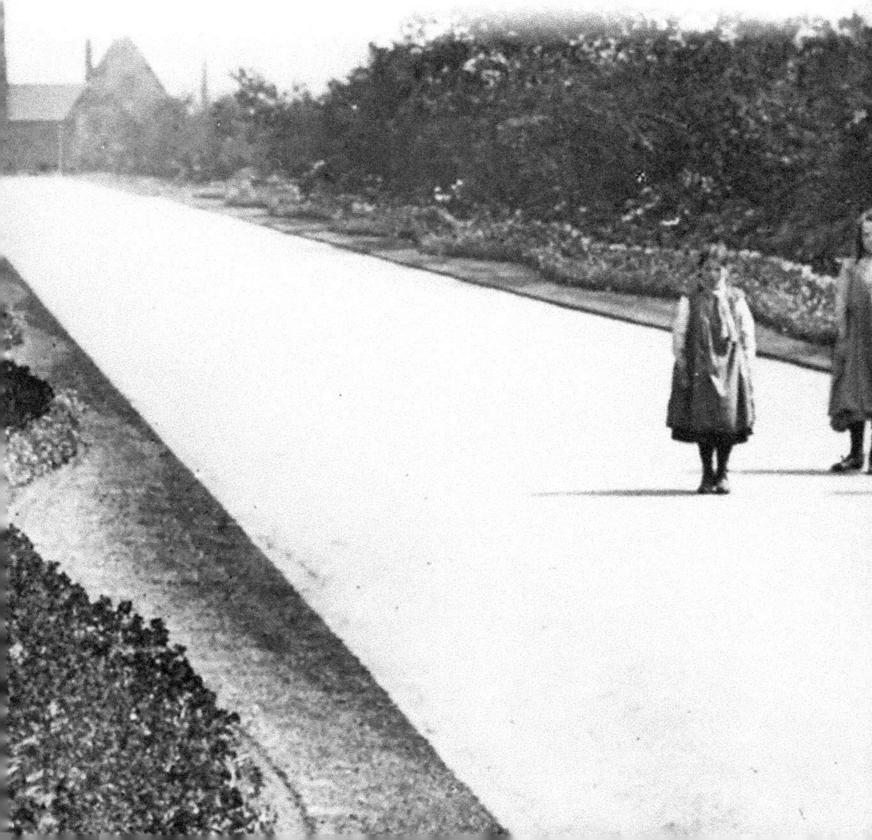

5. THE LAKES, *c.* 1930

Two of Hebburn's four lakes are clearly seen here. Also called 'Hebburn Hall Ponds', they were reservoirs for local works. Created in the nineteenth century, they are fondly remembered as a picturesque contrast to the surrounding industrial town. The lakes were also used for boating and fishing, and in 1907 they were described as a wildlife haven 'teeming with trout'. Drained by 1968, schools and houses now stand in their place.

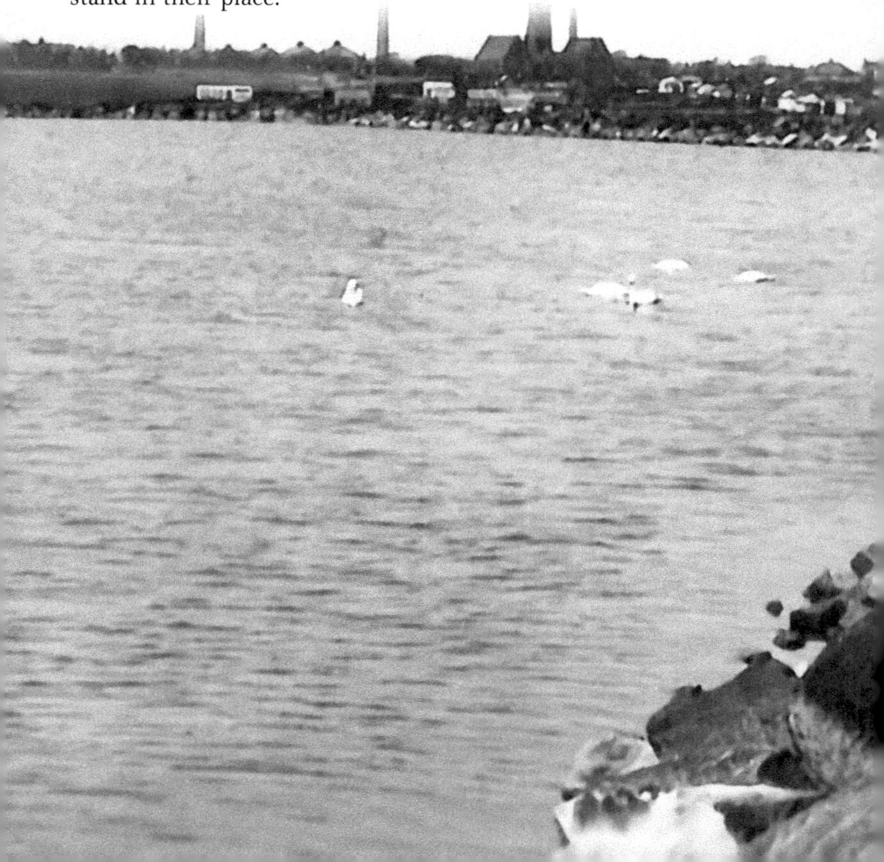

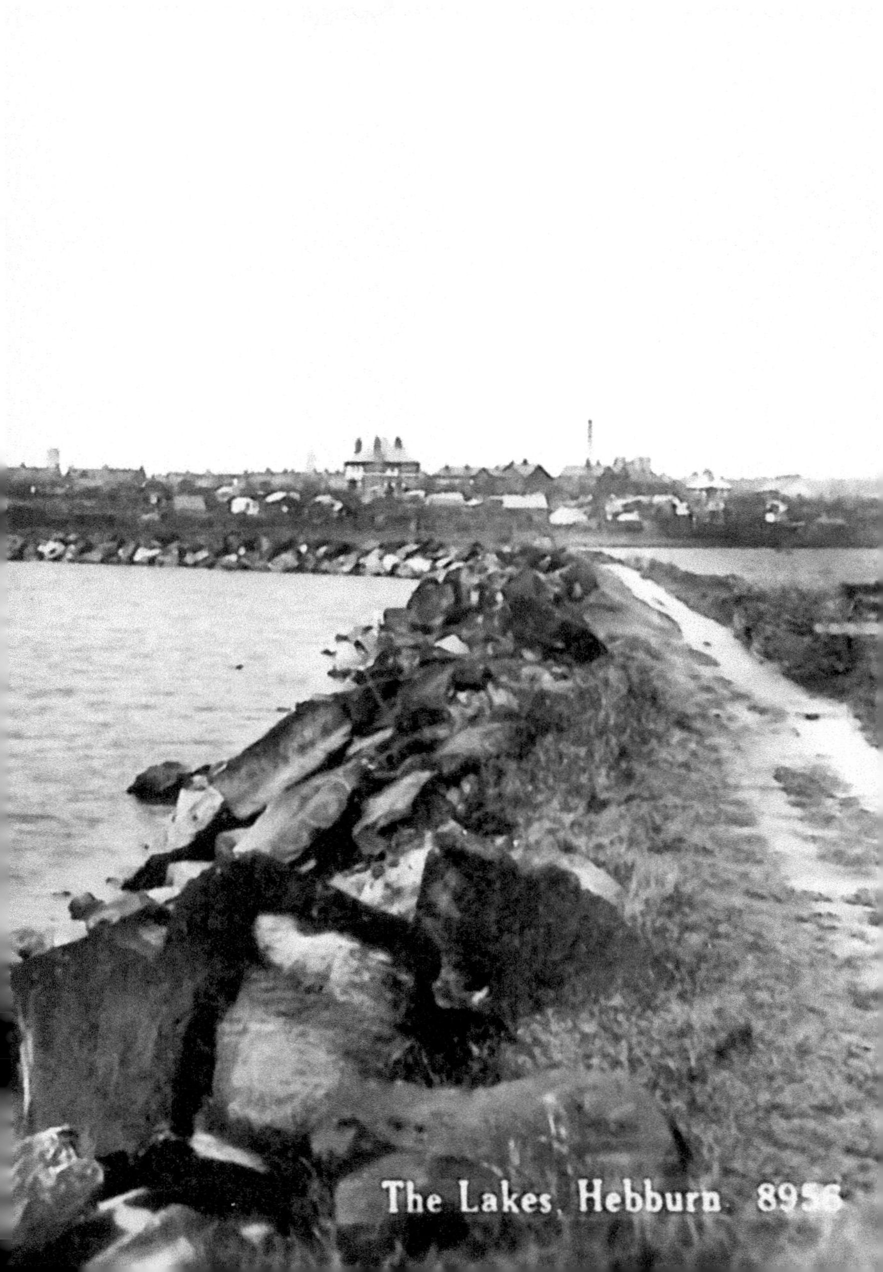
The Lakes, Hebburn 8956

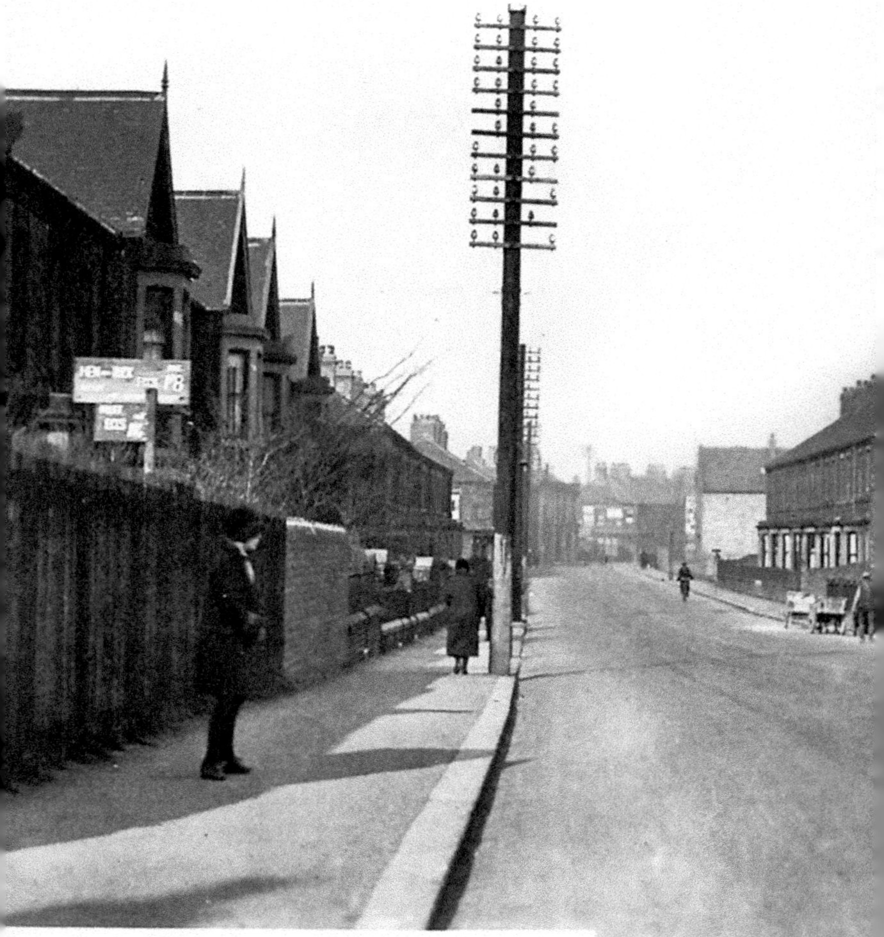

Newton Terrace, Hebburn. 8952

6. VICTORIA ROAD WEST AND NEWTON TERRACE, *c.* 1930

Victoria Road, Hebburn's 'high road', follows a traditional east–west route between Newcastle and South Shields, though it has been slightly diverted around Hebburn Hall since the eighteenth century. Finishing touches are being applied to semi-detached houses on the right, while on the left – the site of North Farm – fresh eggs are for sale. Patches of countryside remained in Hebburn during the 1930s, and a large tree at the roadside is a reminder of that rural past.

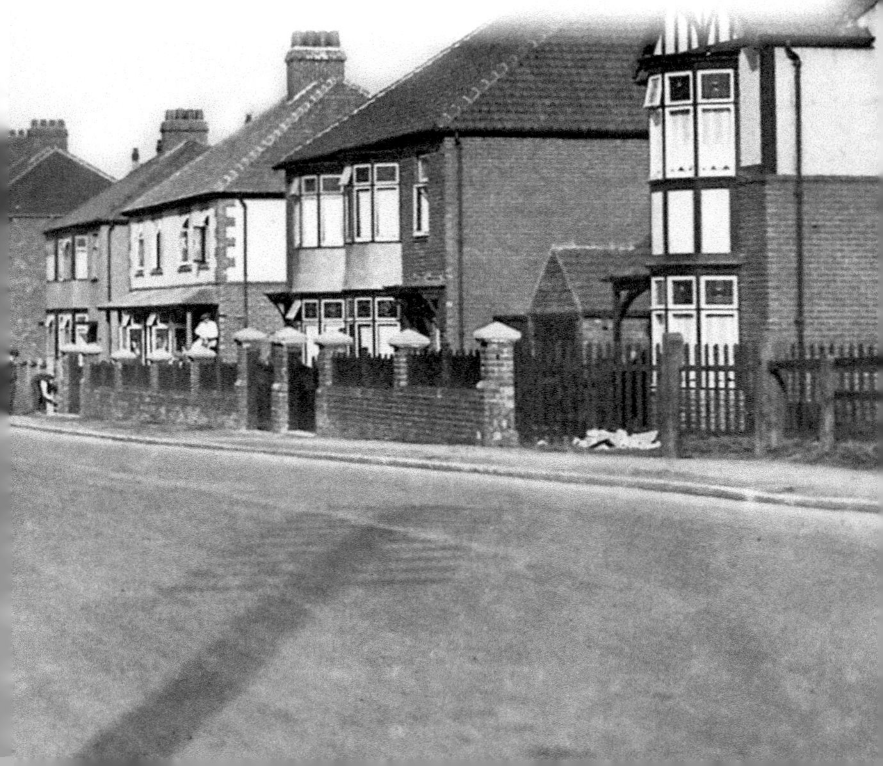

7. TENNANT STREET, *c.* 1930

History is often revealed through street names. Charles Tennant's chemical company began at Hebburn riverside in 1864 and later Newtown's Tennant Street, where many factory workers lived, became a bustling mix of shops and houses. Putt's tobacconist (afterwards Murray's newsagent) displays its sign and nearby hang the three balls of Davison's pawnbroker – a true sign of the times. Following construction in the 1960s of the flats and shopping centre, only the distinctive outline of Aln Street Masonic Club (built in 1925) remains in the background to connect present to past.

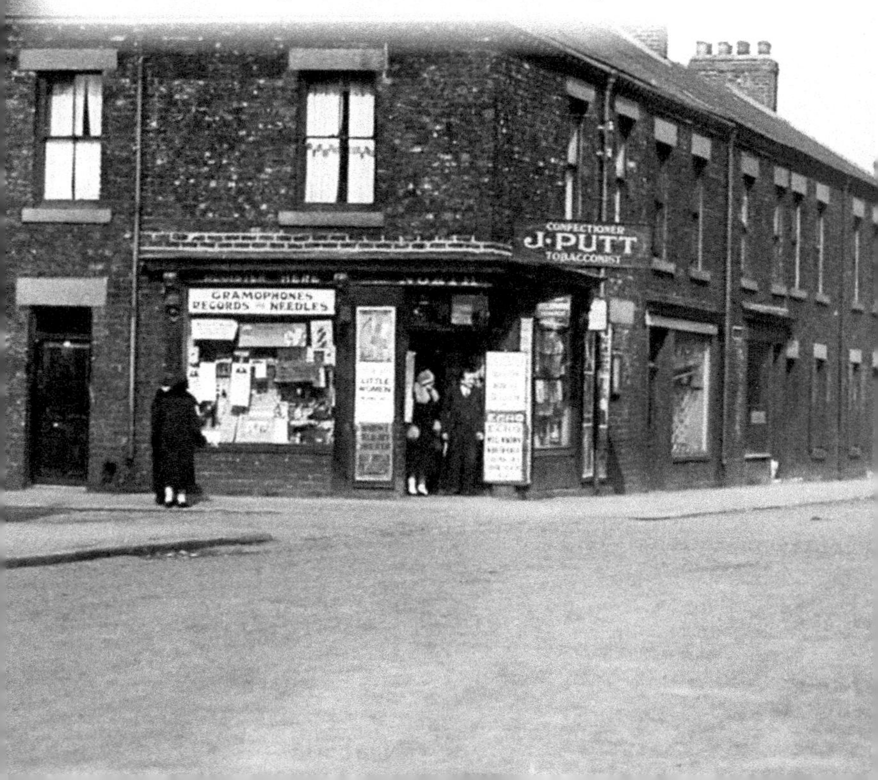

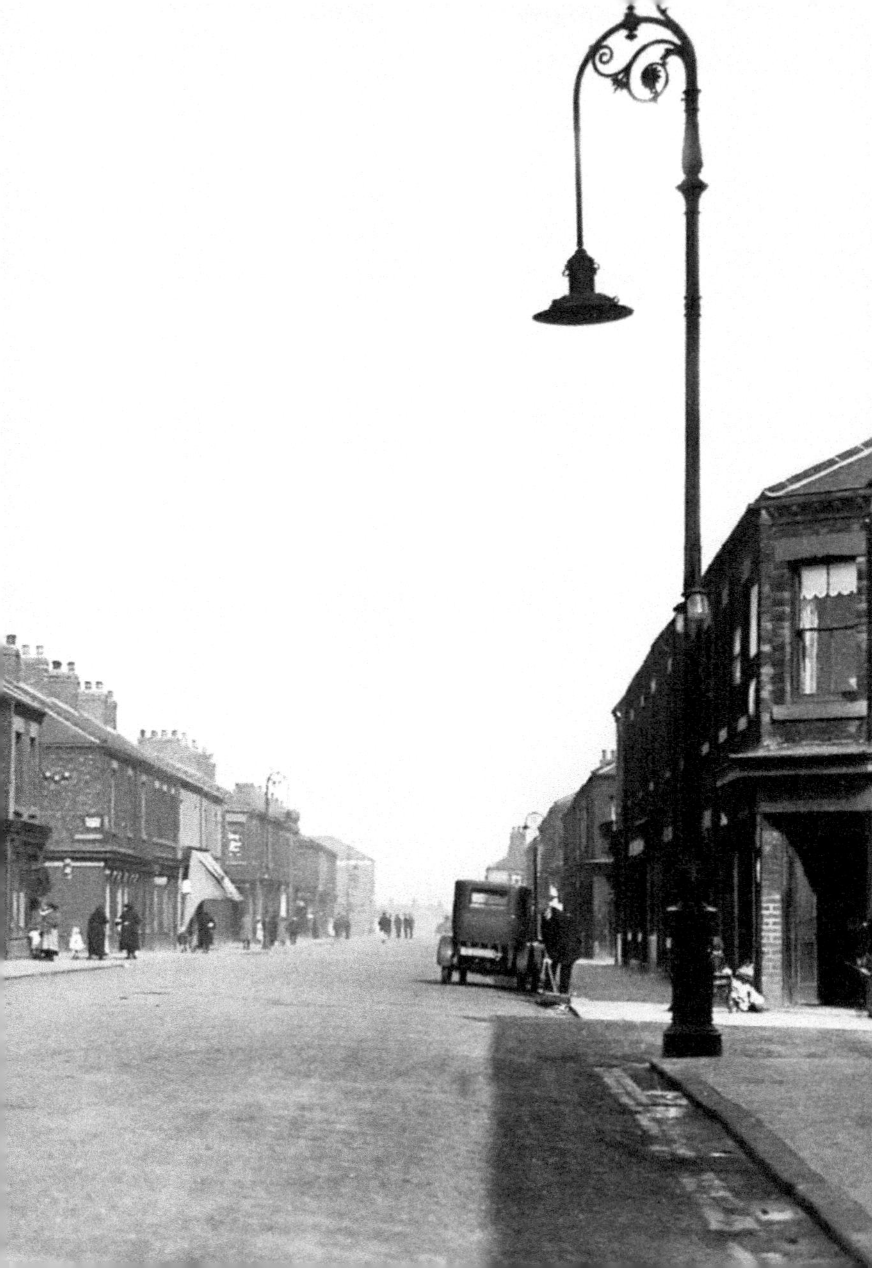

8. AMBULANCE HALL, VICTORIA ROAD WEST, *c.* 1930

St John's Ambulance Association was established in 1887 and a Hebburn branch was formed shortly afterwards. By 1902 it had over thirty members and training sessions were conducted by local doctors in private houses. The Ambulance Hall opened in 1926, appropriately enough on the corner of St John's Avenue and Victoria Road, and was equipped with a garage, used by the taxi company that formerly occupied the building.

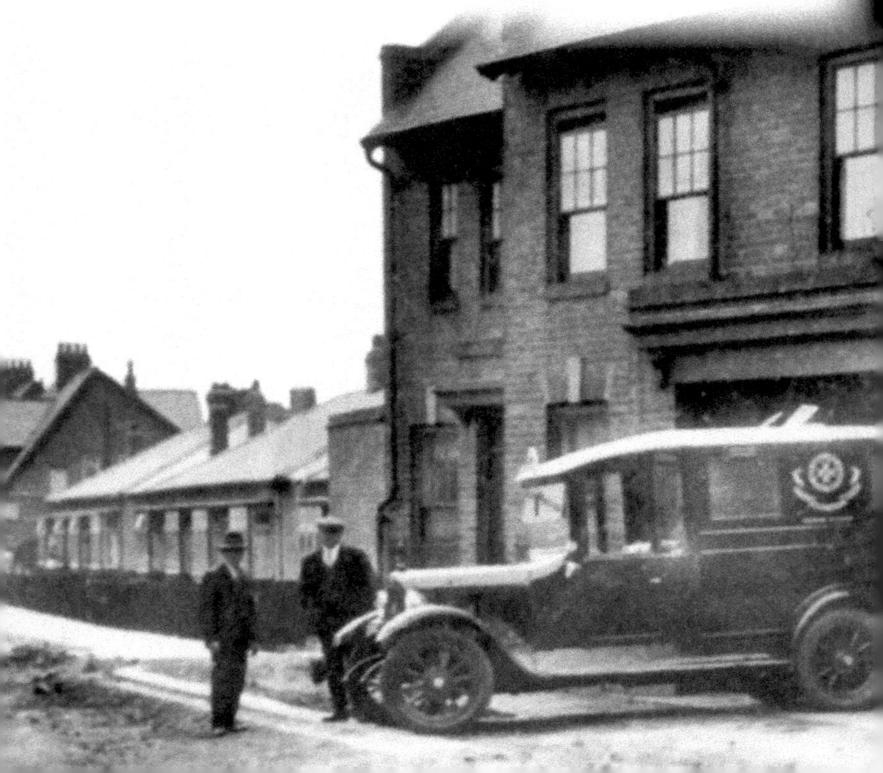

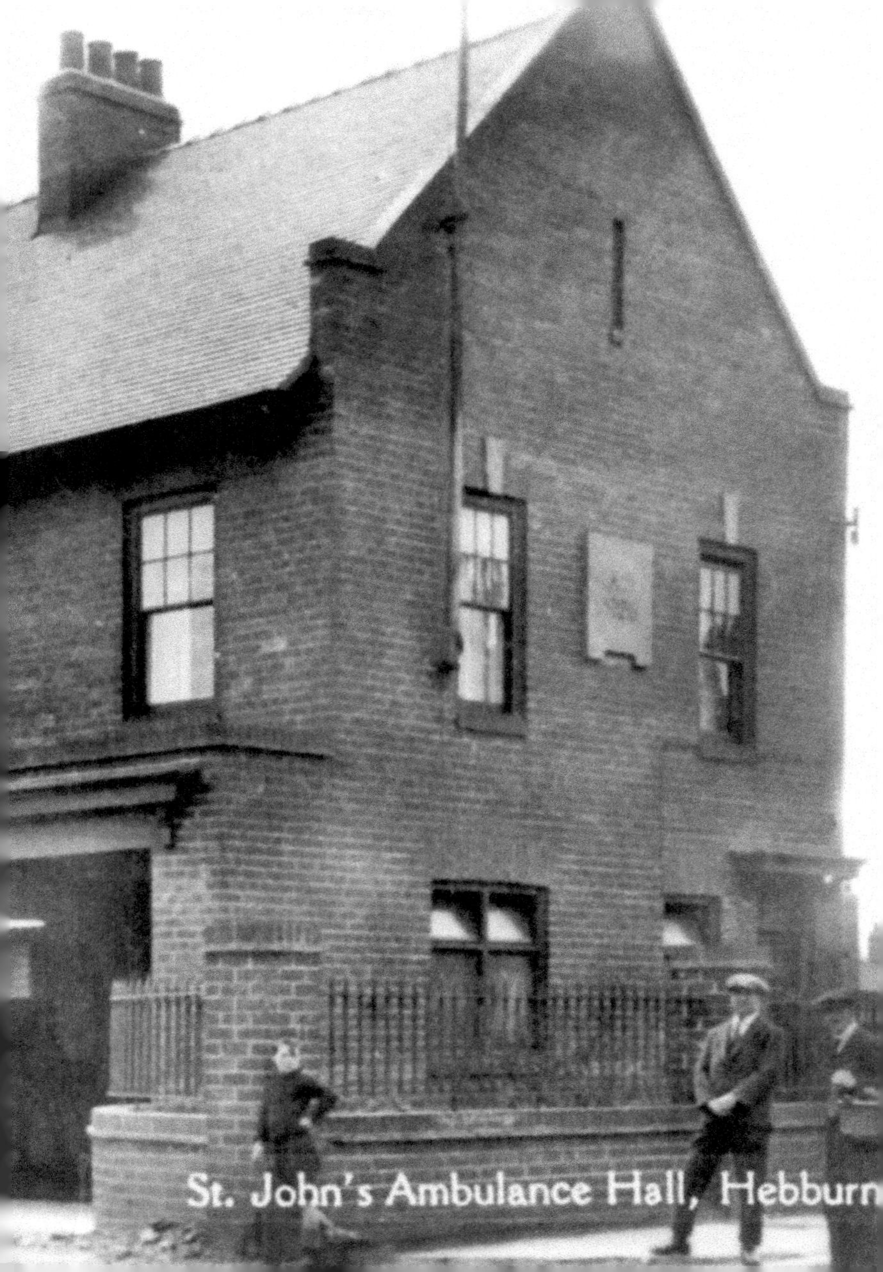
St. John's Ambulance Hall, Hebburn

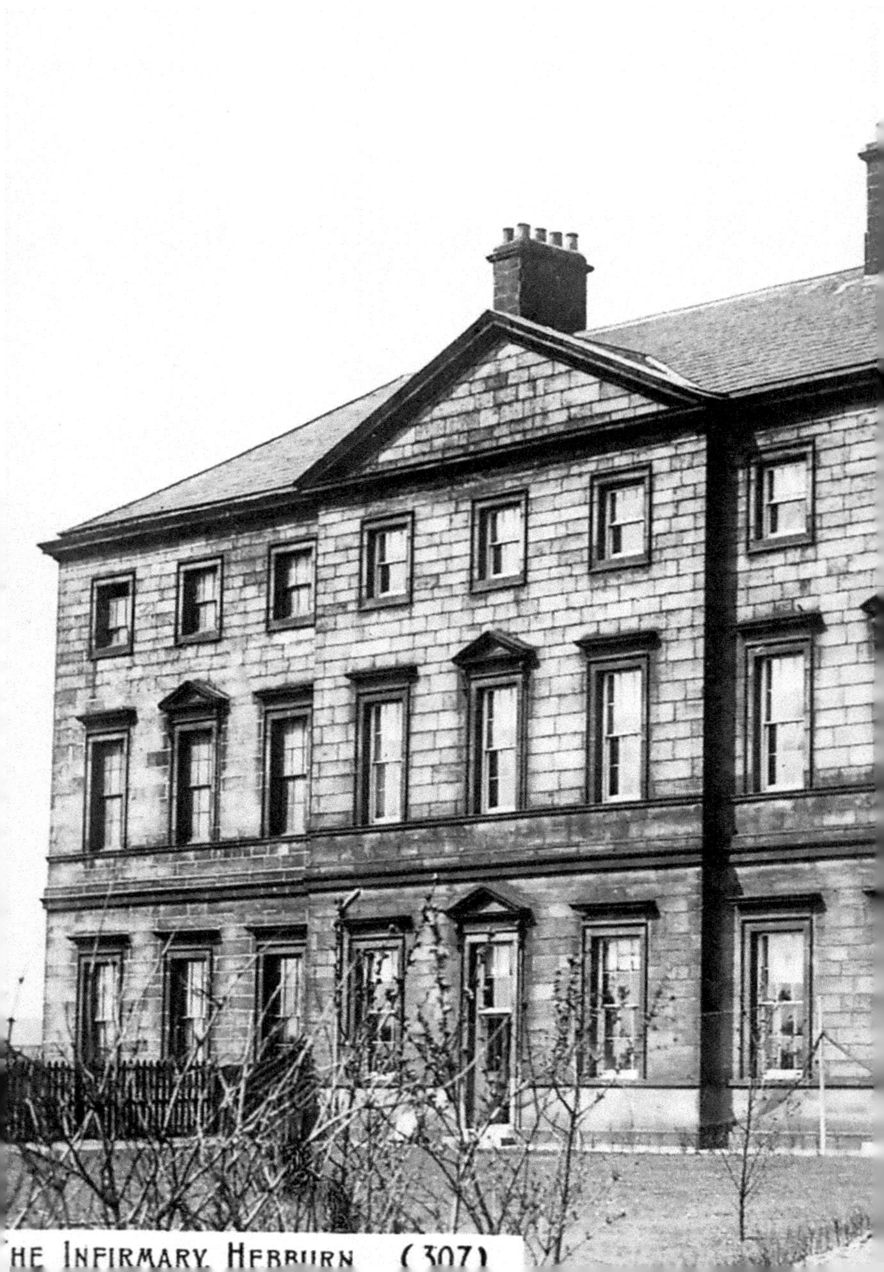
HE INFIRMARY, HEBBURN (307)

9. HEBBURN HALL (ELLISON HALL), *c.* 1905

Hebburn Hall has changed greatly over the centuries. Originally a medieval tower, it became an Elizabethan mansion before the Ellison family transformed it to one of the area's finest classically styled buildings. Newcastle architect William Newton is believed to have designed the present Hebburn Hall. Within thirty years it was superficially altered, this time by John Dobson. Two centuries on – despite a screen of trees – the grandeur of the hall's south front remains plain to see.

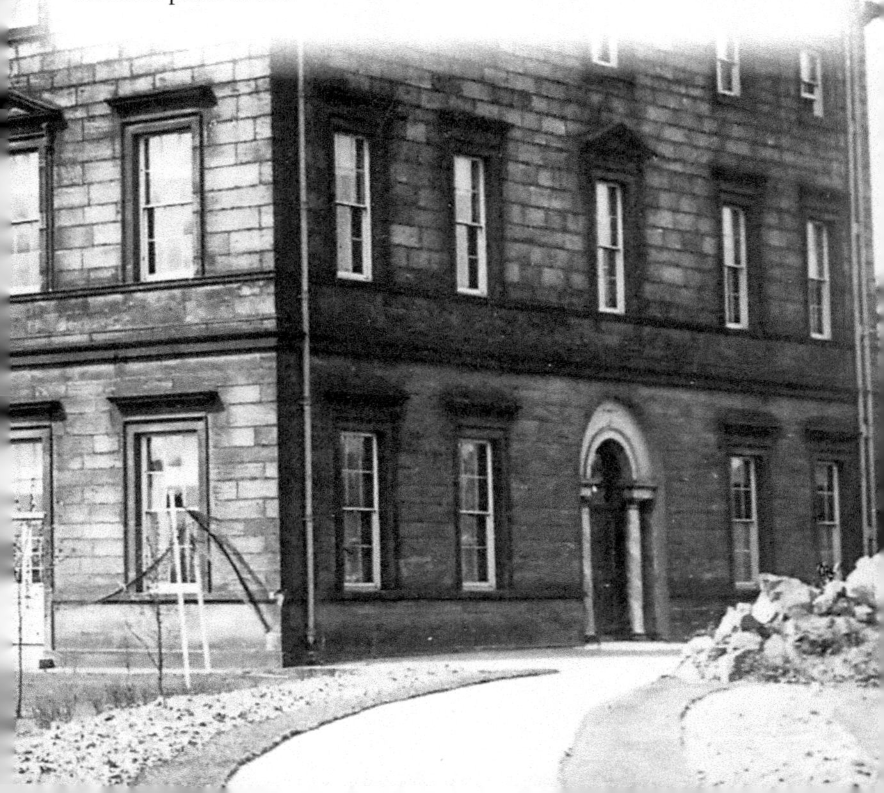

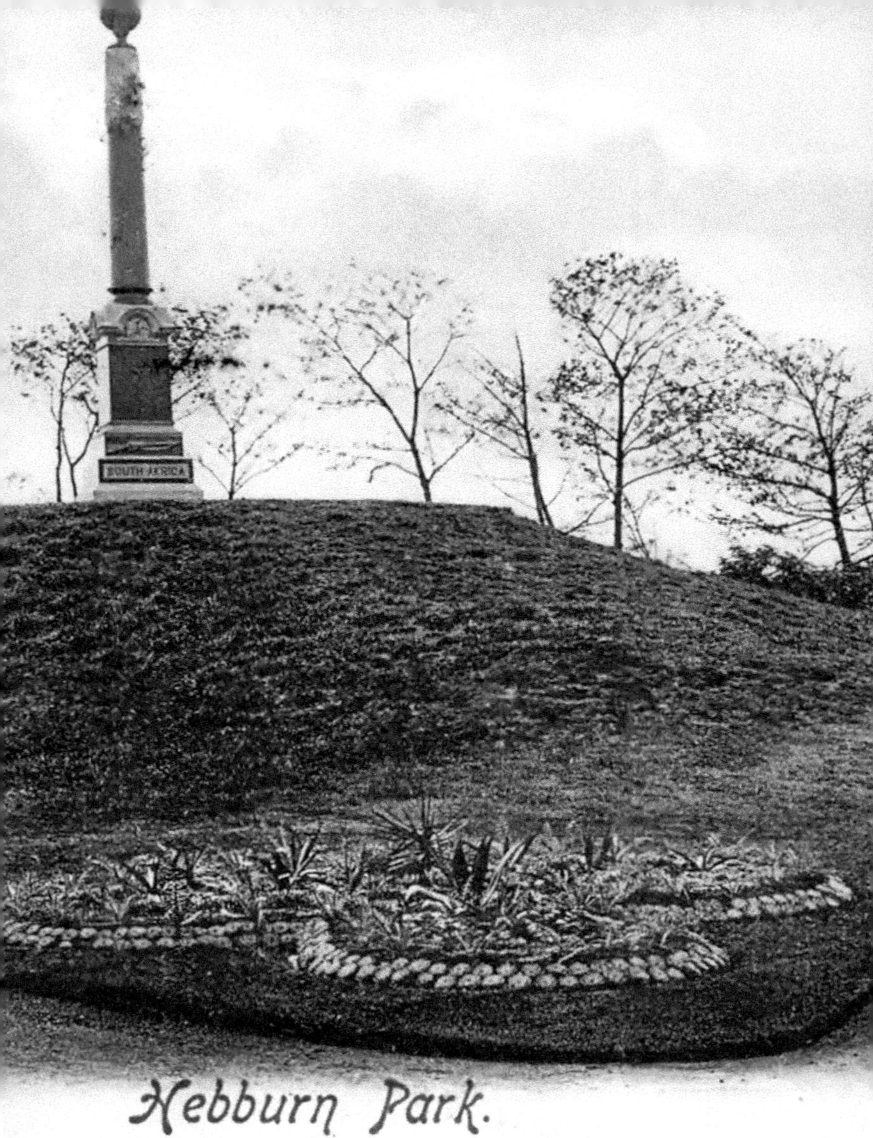

Hebburn Park.

he Wrench Series, No. 7743.

10. BOER WAR MEMORIAL, *c.* 1903

Hebburn servicemen killed in South Africa in 1899/1902 are commemorated in Carr Ellison Park. Six names are inscribed on the Boer War memorial, which is a tall granite column set on a triple pedestal. It stands on a mound next to the 'Dene' – previously a sunken garden in Hebburn Hall and before that an ornamental pond. The monument continues to be a magnet for local children who play on the miniature cannon next to it.

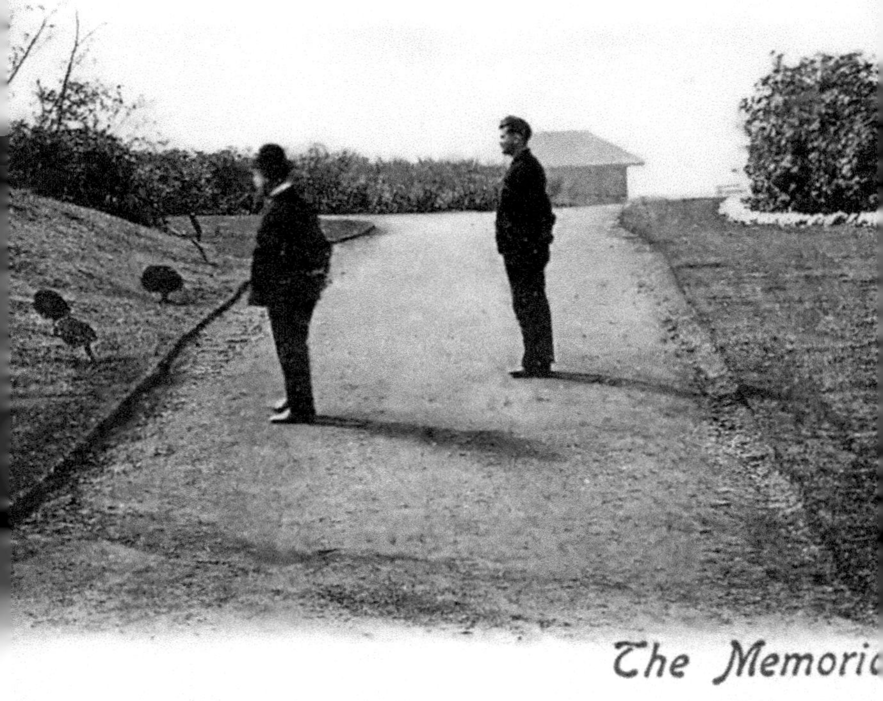

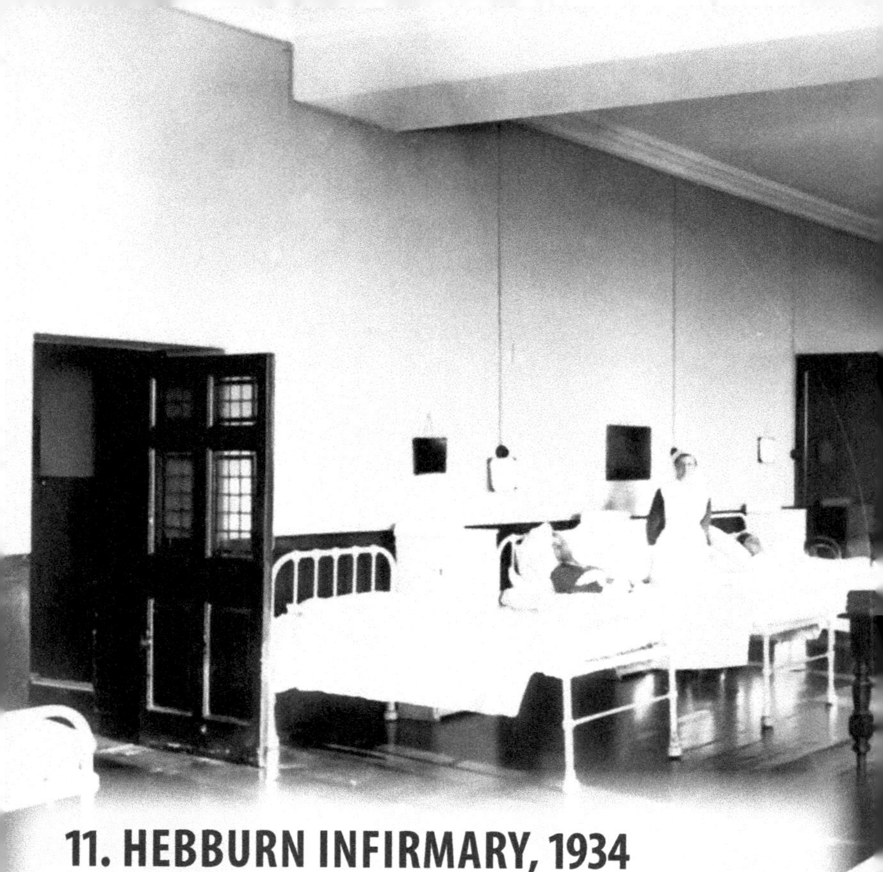

11. HEBBURN INFIRMARY, 1934

A local metalworker was the first patient to be treated at Hebburn Infirmary when it opened in August 1898. Before then casualties were taken to Newcastle, but Ralph Carr Ellison allowed part of Hebburn Hall to become a hospital and by 1914 the publicly funded institution was equipped with emergency wards and X-ray facilities. From 1966 until its closure in 1976 the infirmary housed a geriatric unit and now, after conversion to luxury apartments, fee-paying guests occupy the former wards.

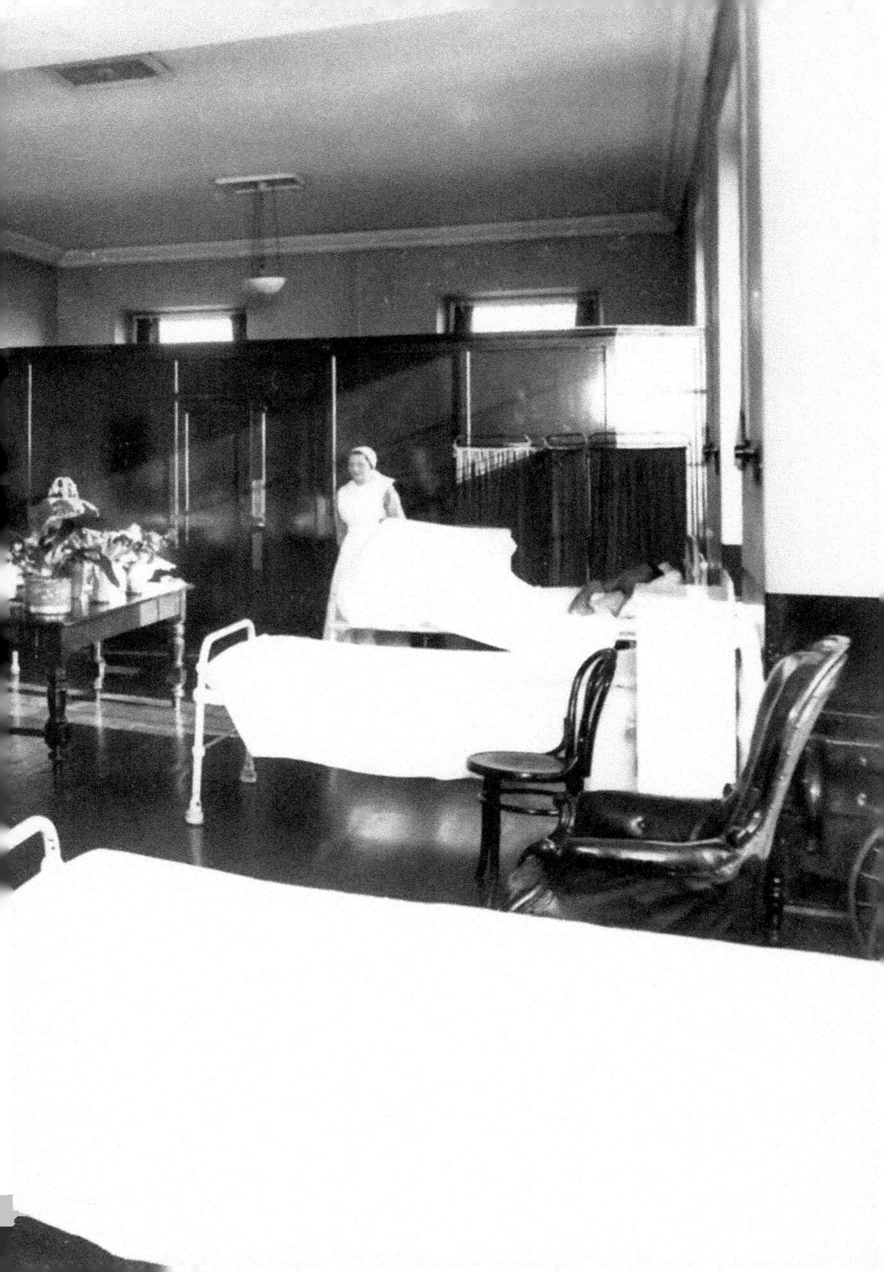

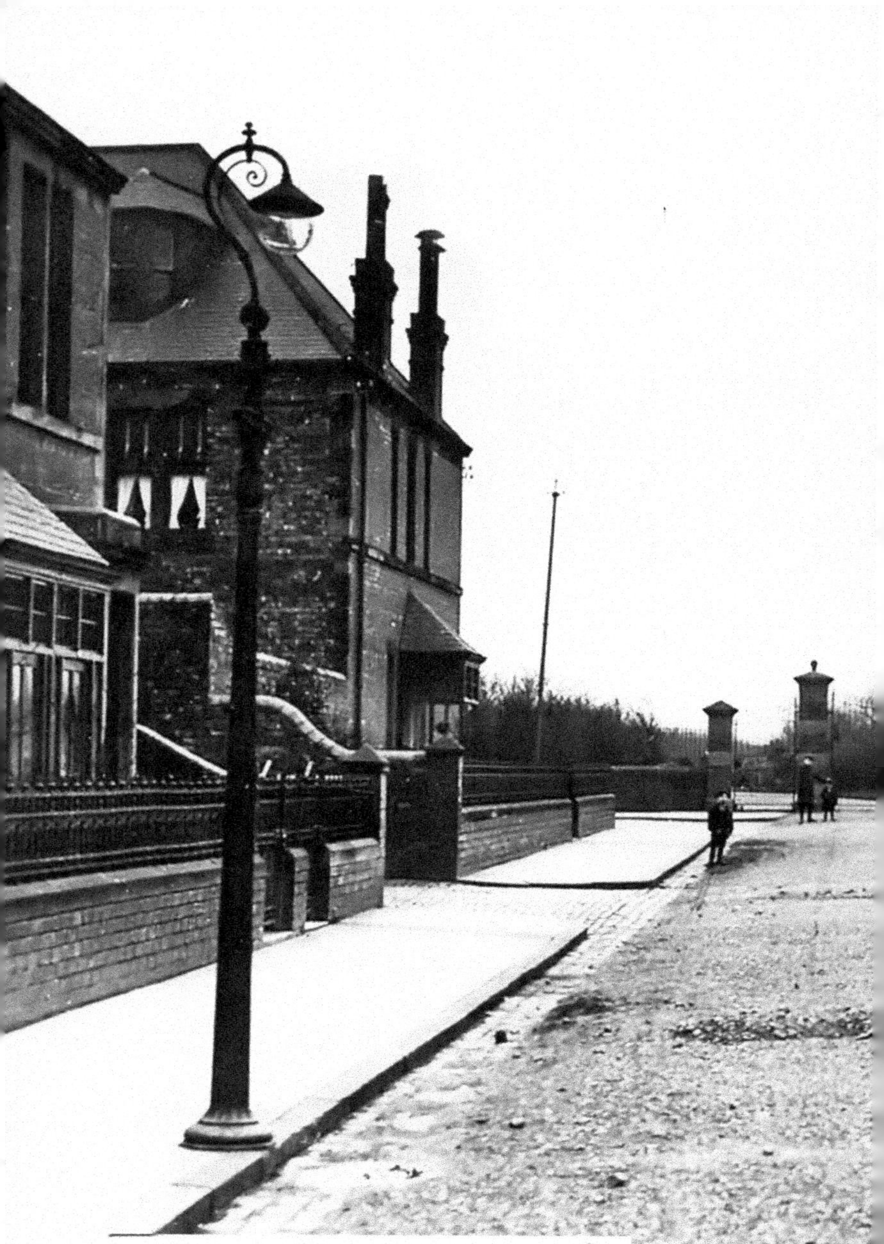

PARK GATES, HEBBURN 412

12. PARK ROAD, *c.* 1910

Park Road was relatively new when this photograph was taken. These spacious late Victorian and Edwardian terraces were built over former plantations on the old Hebburn Hall estate. A century on little appears to have changed apart from the ubiquitous cars and lost view of the Boer War memorial. Helped by its proximity to Carr Ellison Park the street has retained a visual character and appeal, which were recognised in 2007 when it was included in the Hebburn Hall Conservation Area.

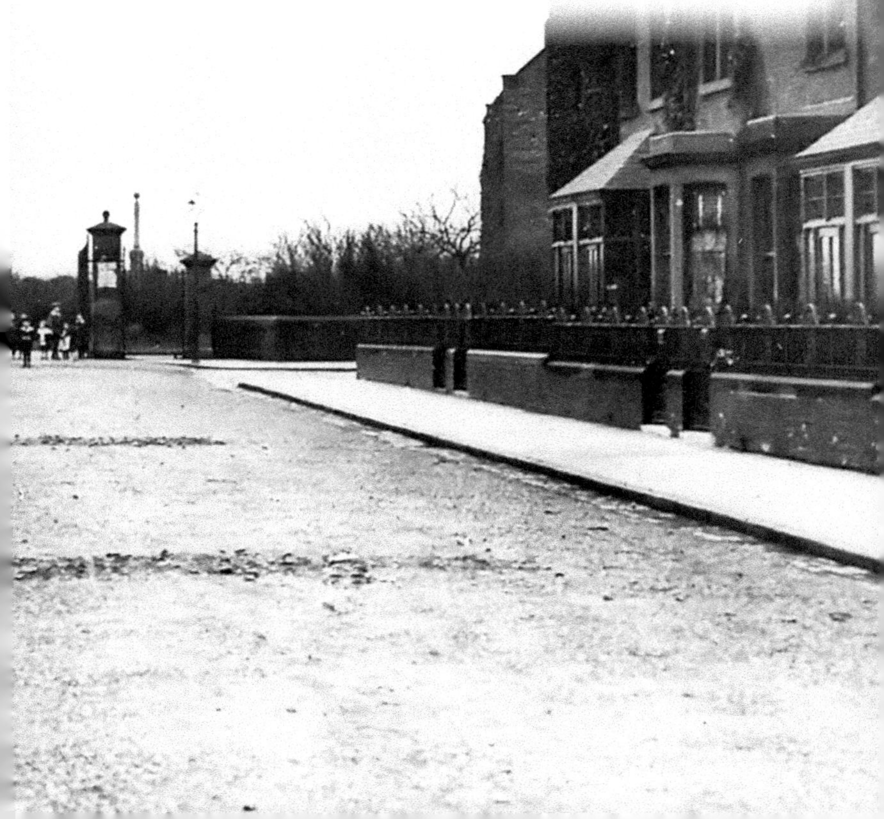

13. SHOPPING CENTRE, ST JOHN'S PRECINCT, 1967

Fresh and bright when it was built in the 1960s, Hebburn's shopping centre has deteriorated like many similar structures of that era. Over the decades shrinking trade and vacated shops have caused the centre to become rundown, making its repair or replacement a major local issue. Hopes for a £40-million redevelopment were dashed in 2010 and though a new community 'hub' has been built, Hebburn town centre continues to wait for a long overdue regeneration.

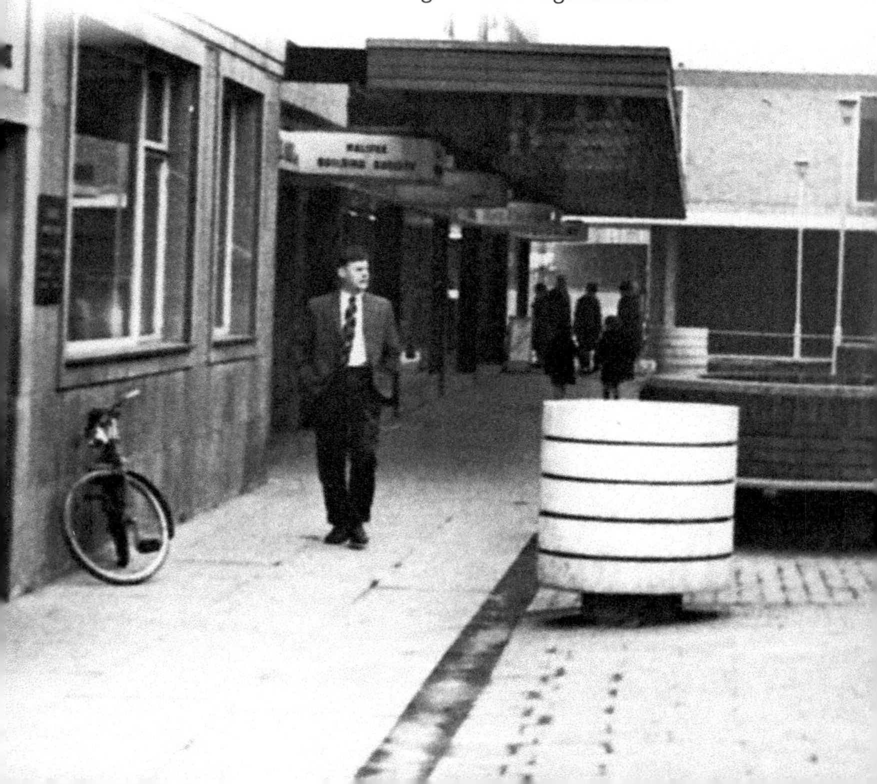

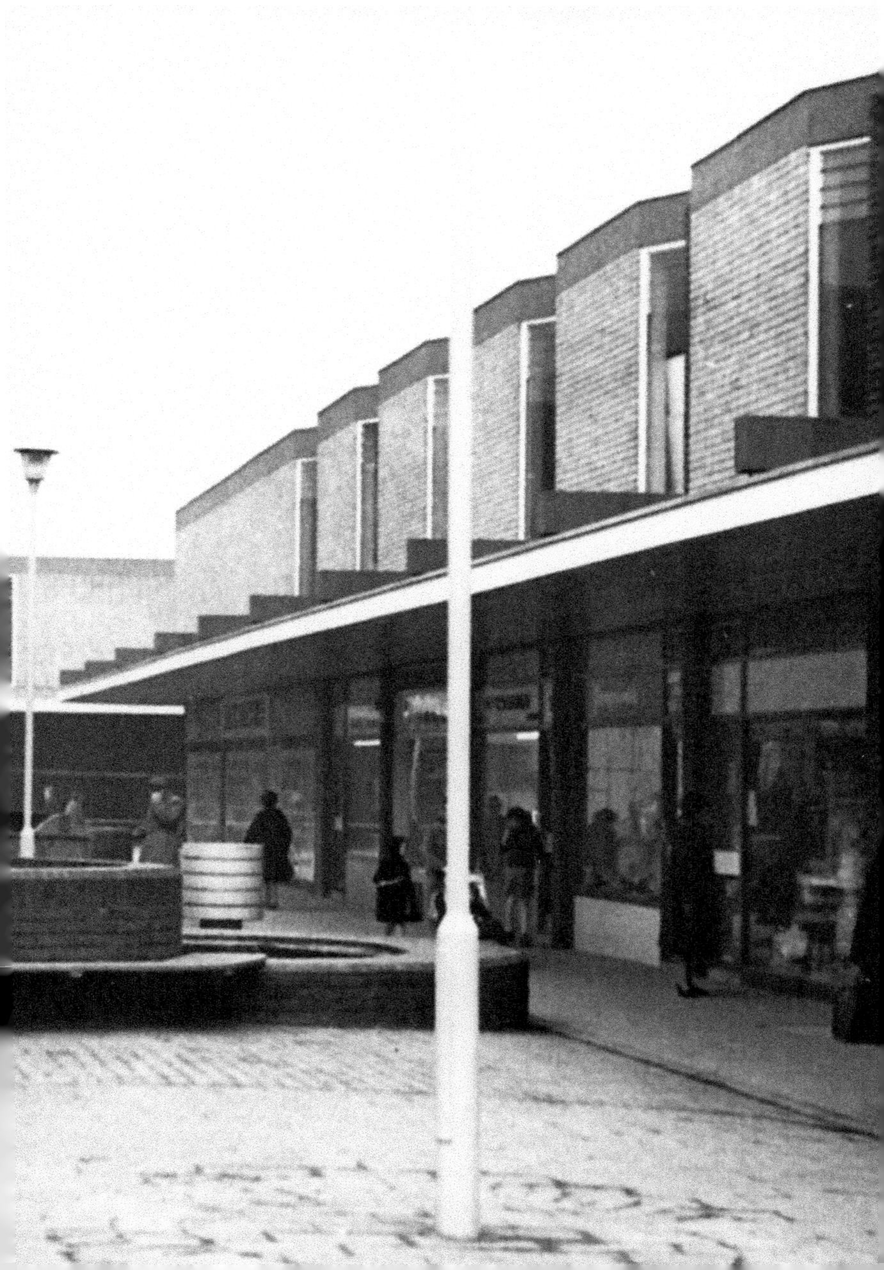

14. VICTORIA ROAD EAST, *c.* 1950

Apart from Hebburn's own skyscraper, Durham Court, the view towards the town's main crossroads appears largely unchanged. Victoria Road East is still lined with substantial terraced houses, but at the traffic lights on the right Hudson's newsagents is now the Black and White barber shop. Across the road, the Protestant Conservative Club, known as the Bentinck, has never surrendered and further along the old Argyle pub, once called Claps and now the Roadhouse, stands empty.

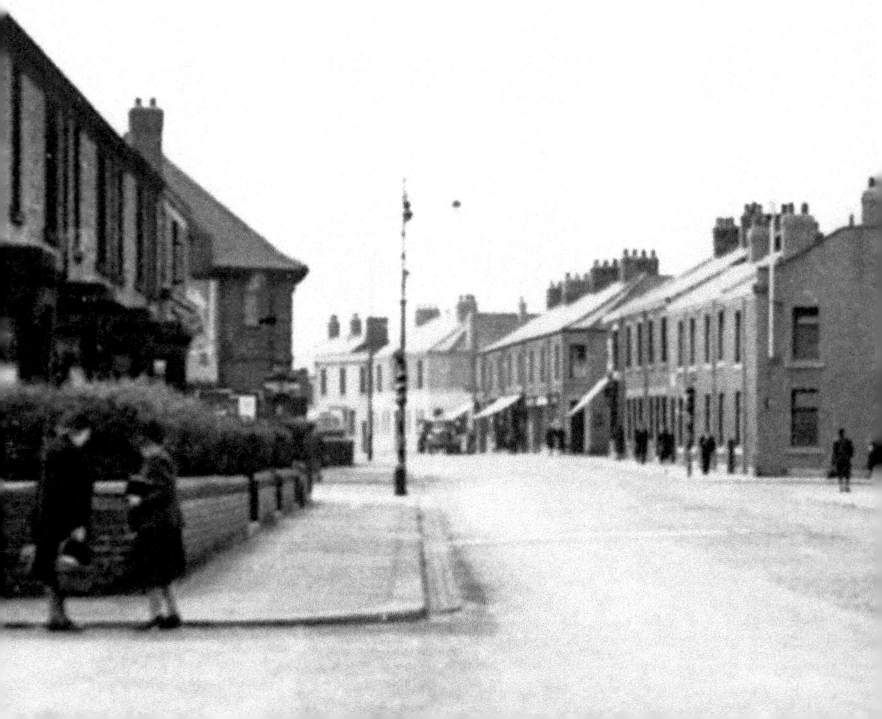

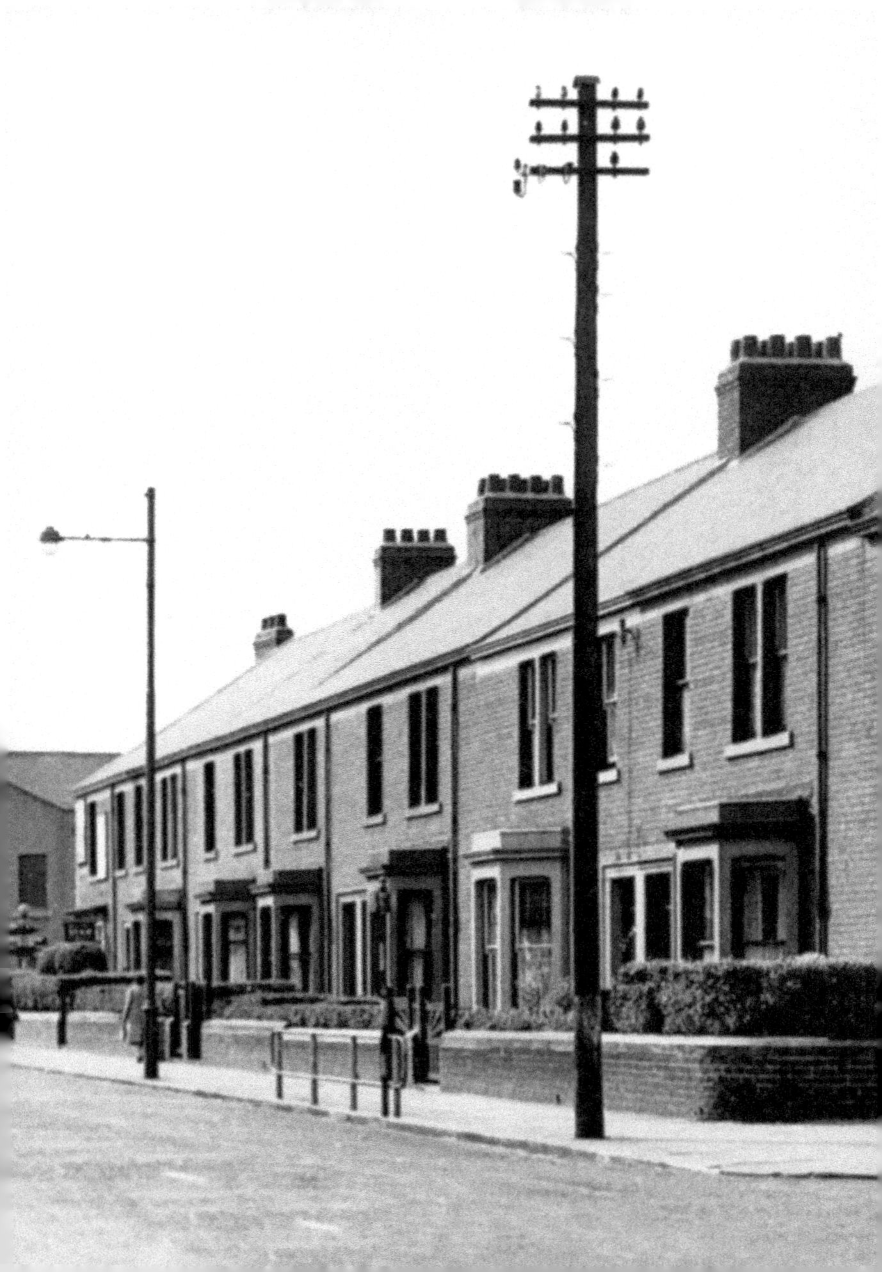

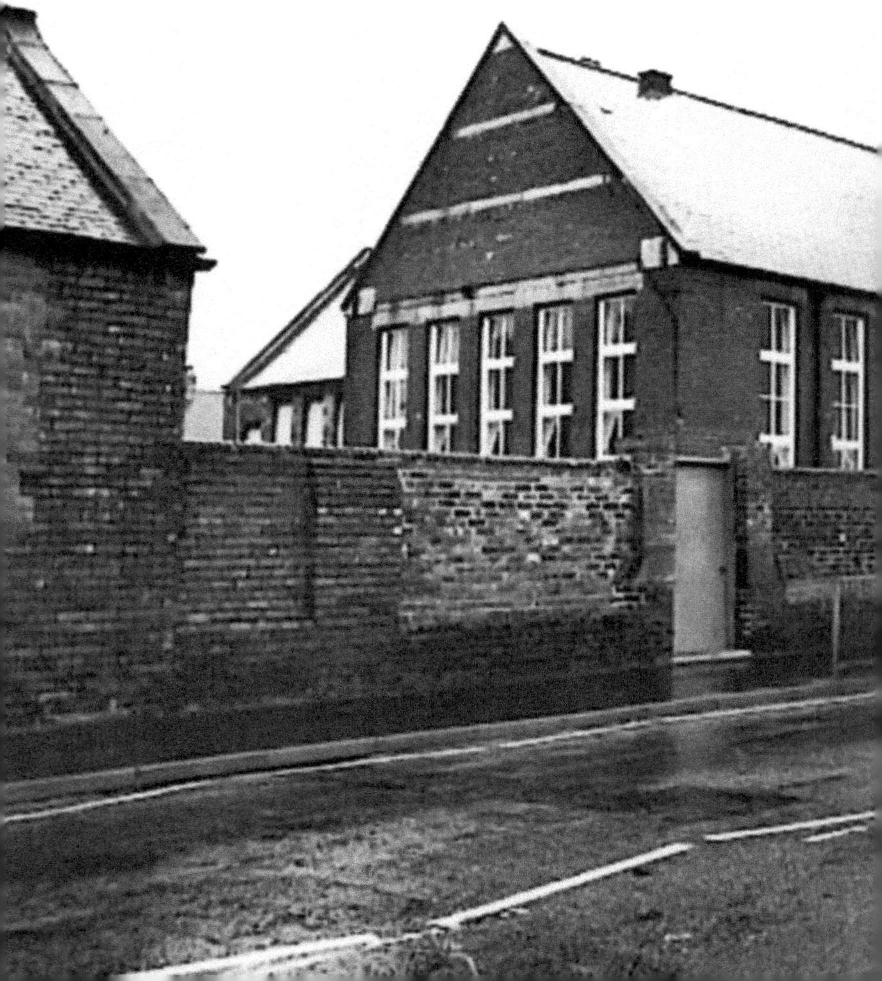

15. NEWTOWN SCHOOL, STATION ROAD, *c.* 1975

Costing £8,000, Hebburn Newtown School opened in May 1875. Established under the Victorian School Board system, it originally housed infants and girls in one section of the building, and boys in the other. After the construction of Clegwell Senior's in the 1930s the Newtown school became a primary until closure in 1984, when pupils were transferred to the renamed Bedewell on Coleridge Square. Landscaped by South Tyneside Council in 1989, the site is now Fountain Square Park.

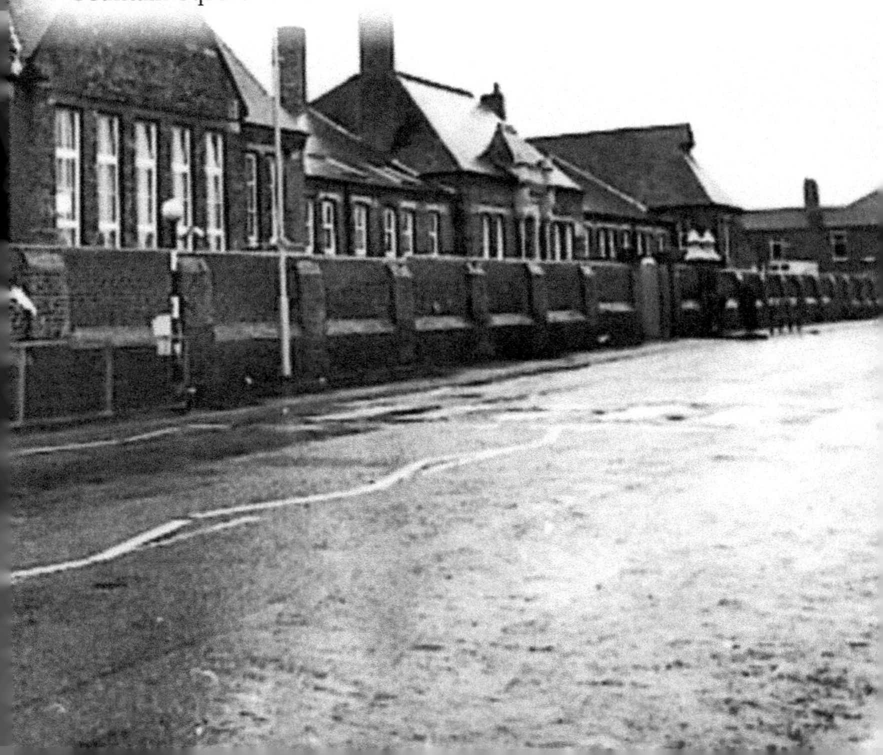

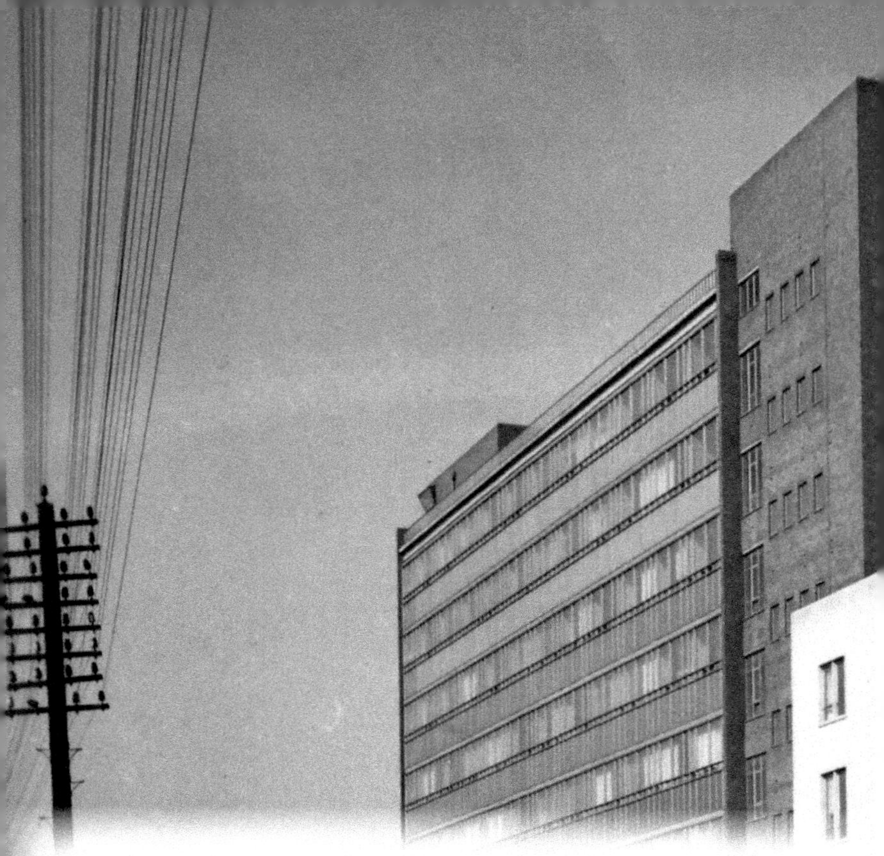

16. REYROLLE OFFICE BLOCK, 1962

Reyrolle's new HQ was built in 1959 at the height of the company's success. It dwarfed the adjacent old buildings, had high-speed lifts and a water- and fireproof basement. Reyrolle was then an internationally renowned manufacturer of switchgear and associated equipment with a workforce of over 10,000, but cutbacks began in 1969 as the company joined in Britain's general industrial decline. Sold to the DHSS a few years later, the Reyrolle offices finally disappeared from the Hebburn skyline in 2010.

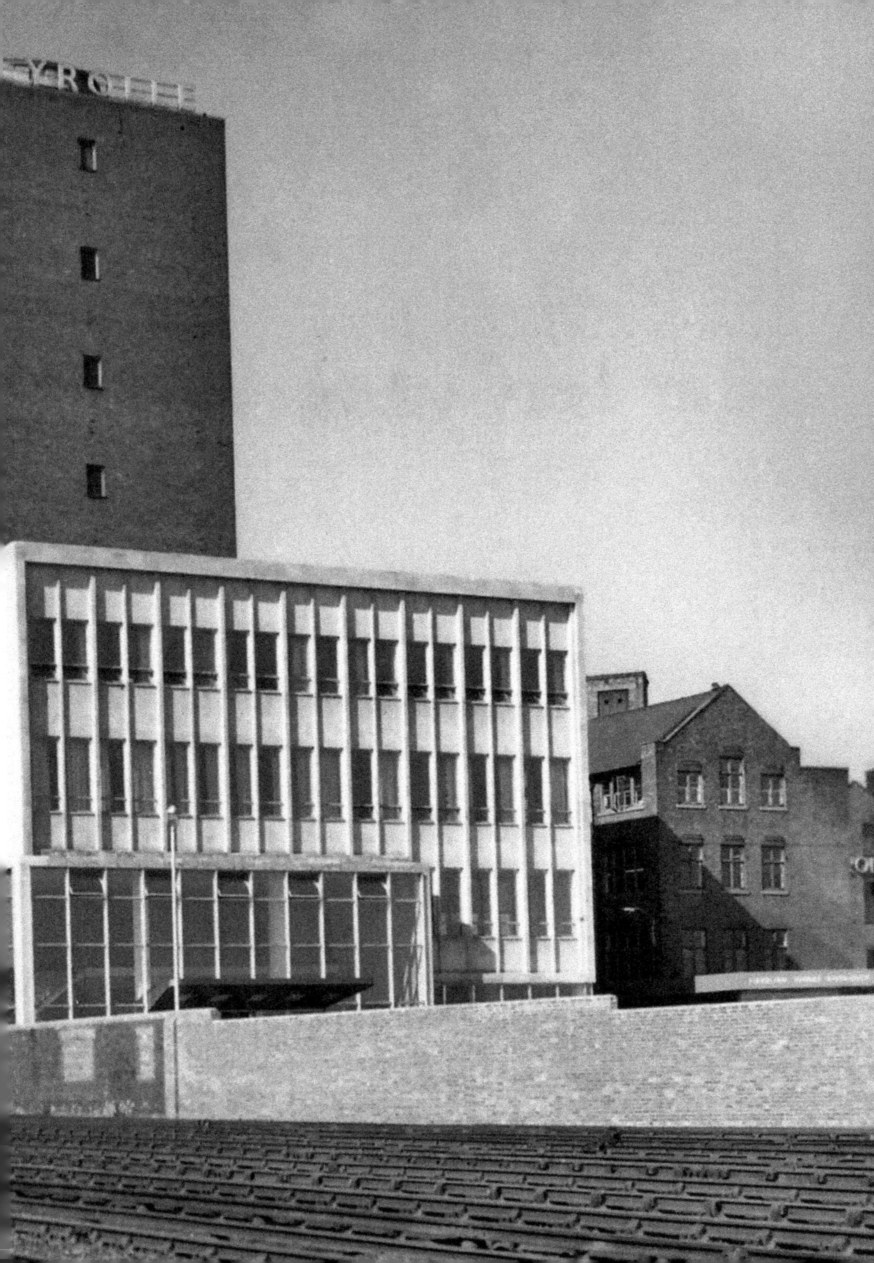

17. REYROLLE, HEBBURN WORKS, *c.* 1910

Alphonse Reyrolle opened his Hebburn factory in May 1901. After establishing a reputation for high-quality engineering in London, the Frenchman began manufacturing electrical equipment in an unused dyeworks near the railway station. With a workforce of around fifty – a number of them from London – Reyrolle responded to a nationwide demand for electrical power and laid the foundation for a business that is connected to Hebburn to this day. The Colour Works site where Reyrolle began is now a housing estate.

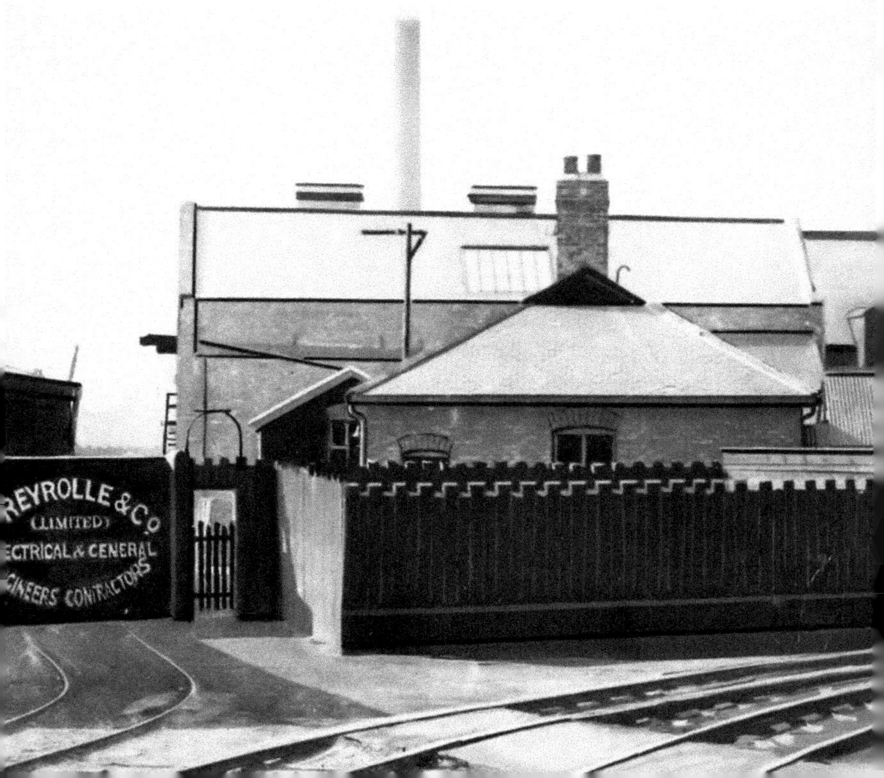

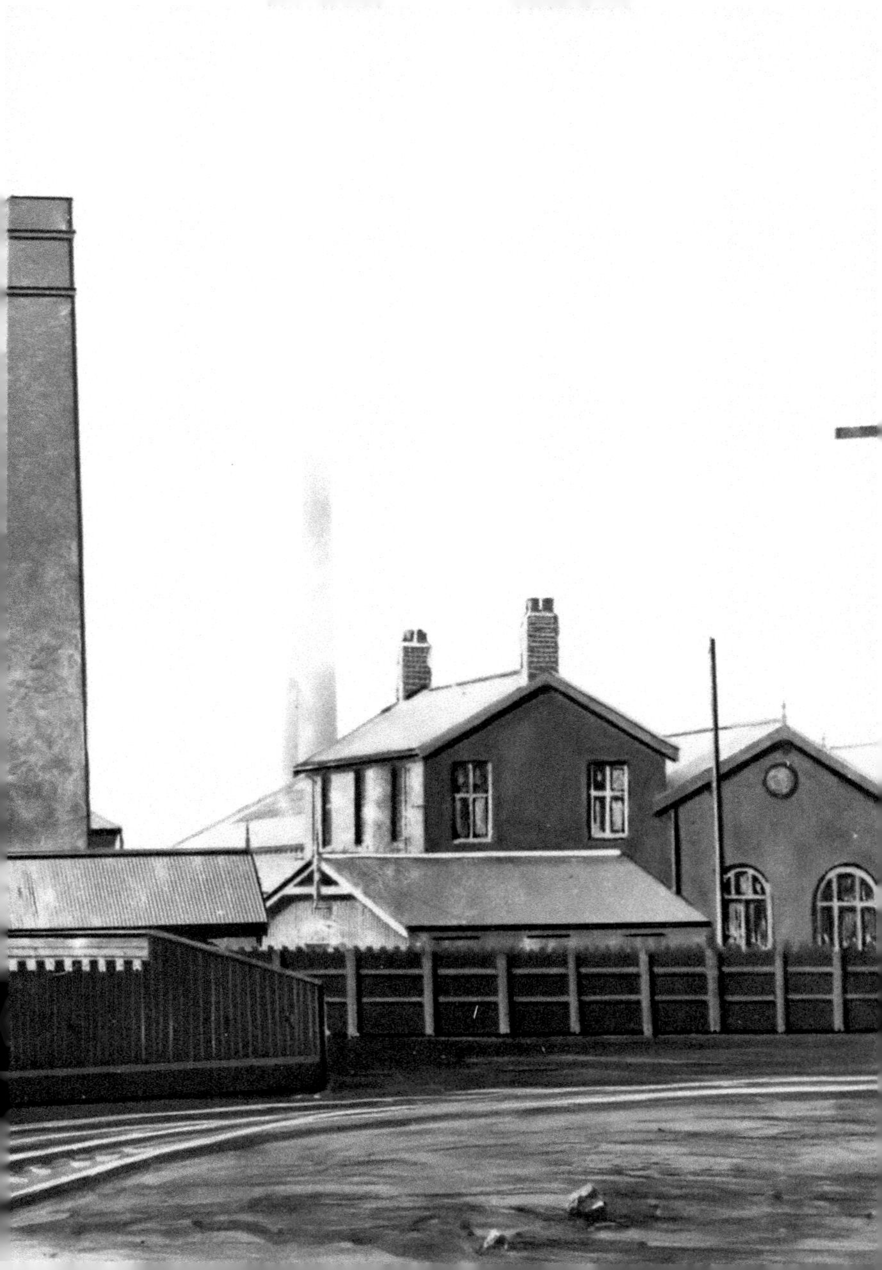

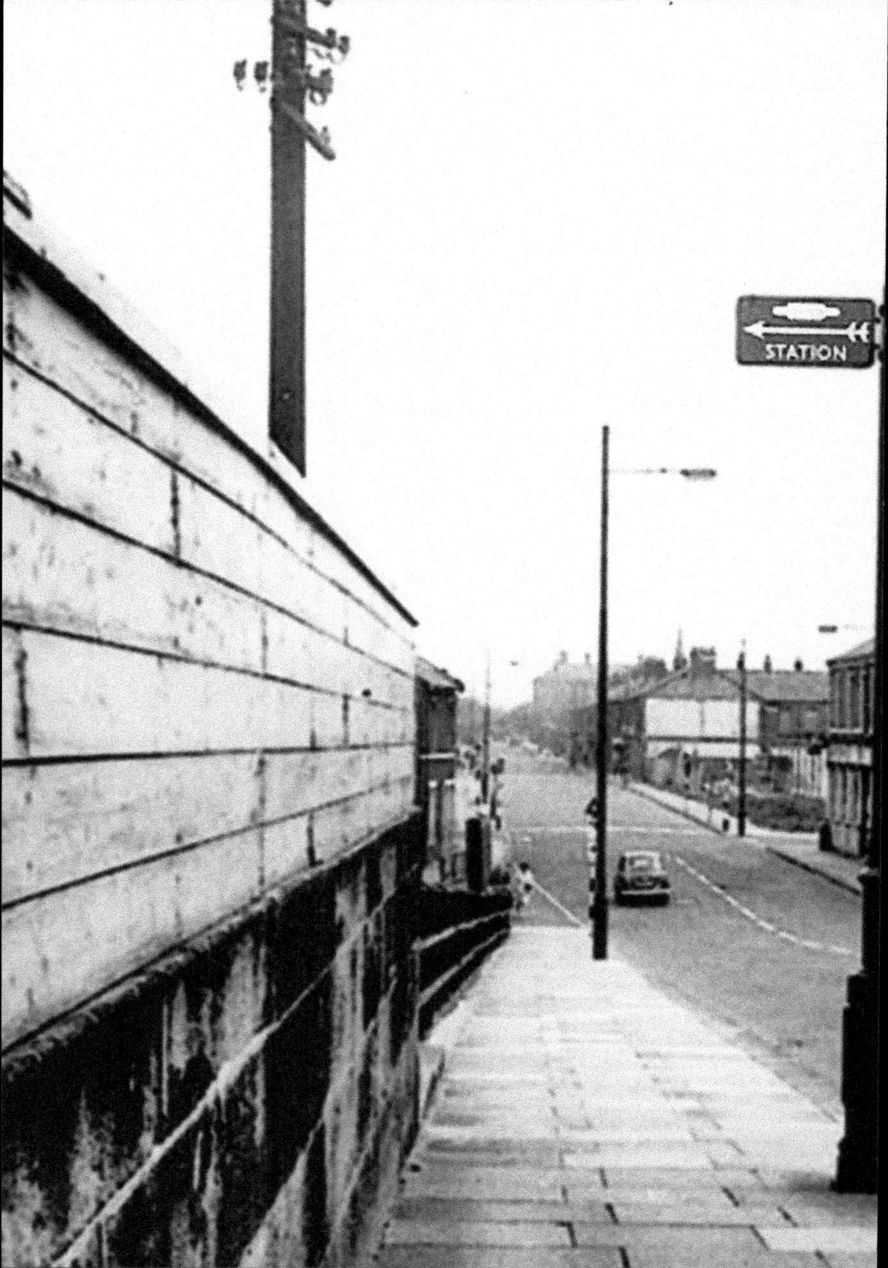
STATION

18. STATION ROAD RAILWAY BRIDGE, 1963

A view from Station Road Bridge shows Newtown in the making. Beyond the Station Hotel (centre right), houses have been torn down for the new shopping centre to come, and Glen Street Wesleyan church is glimpsed (far right). These buildings have gone, but Hebburn Hall and the spire of St John's remain today as distant landmarks.

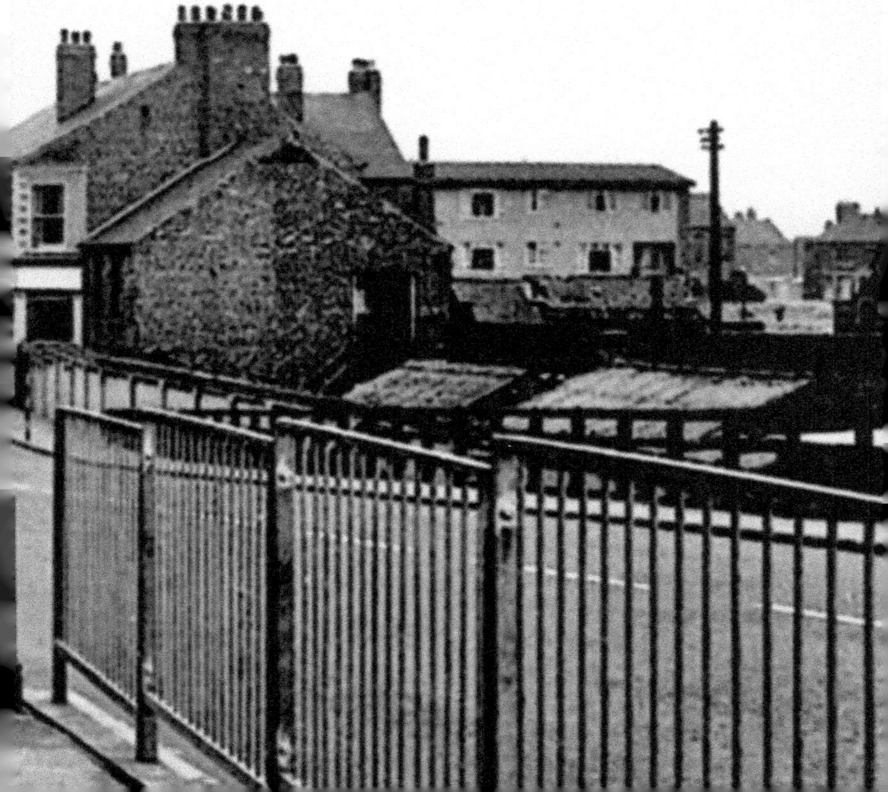

19. RAILWAY STATION, 1965

Most of the Victorian platform buildings pictured here survived until station 'destaffing' in 1969. By 1972 only a few destination boards and antiquated gas lamps remained. But the line survived and the station prospered with the construction of the Metro. Reopened in 1984 with a second platform to the west, Hebburn's new, streamlined station is now a busy part of Tyneside's successful light-rail system.

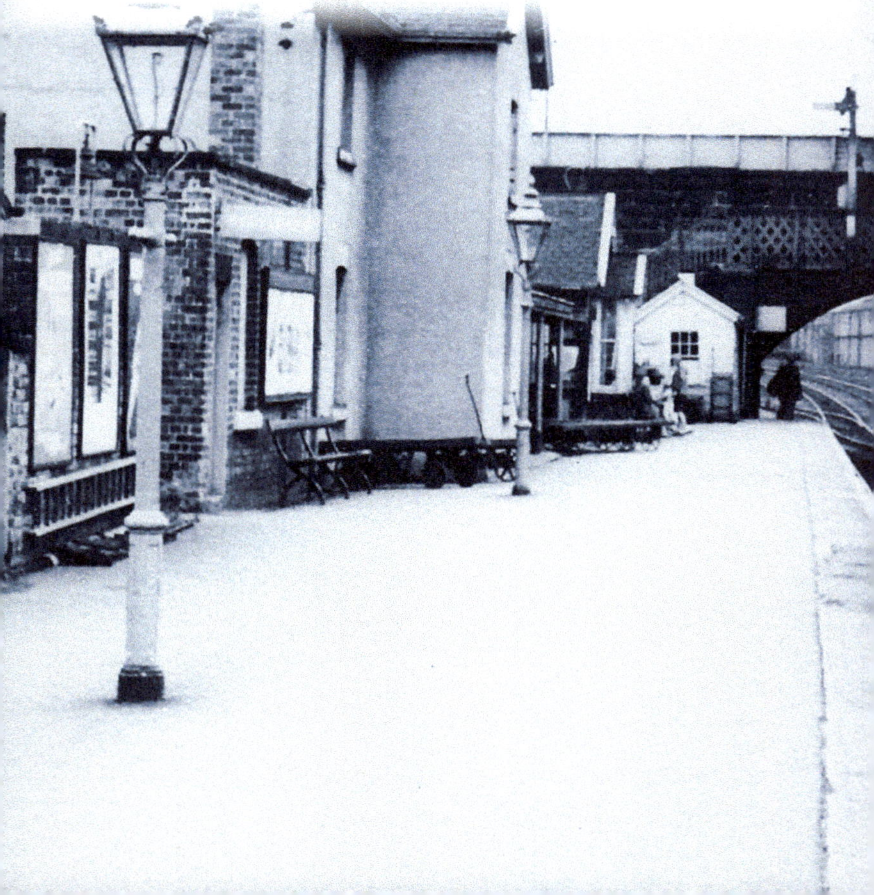

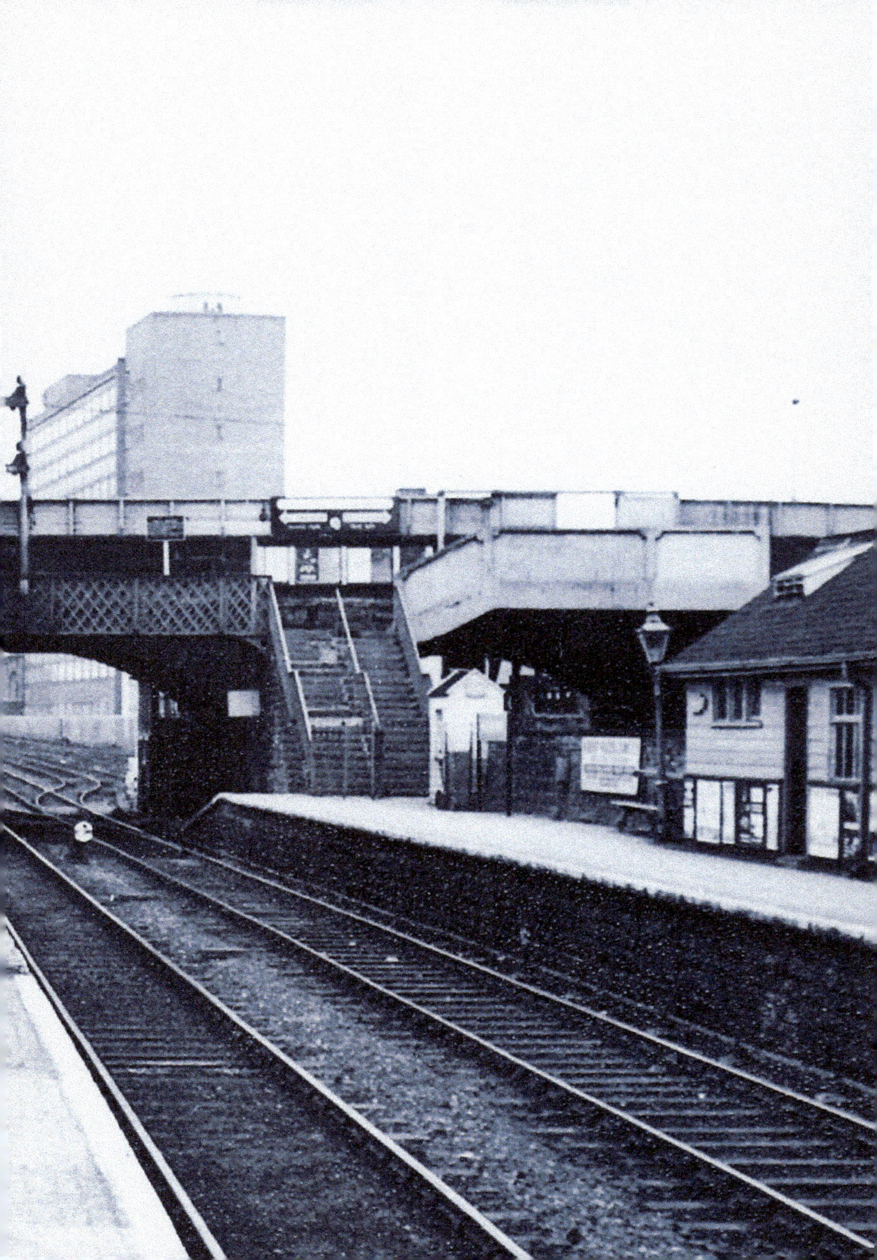

20. FRAZER'S *c.* 1965

In 1889, Newcastle-based Robert Frazer & Sons established their Hebburn business next to the railway, on a plot previously used for sailcloth and rope making. Because of the industrial lubricants the company supplied, it was known initially as the 'grease works', but it built a reputation on structural engineering and steel supply. Nearly 150 years later, present owners Phoenix Steel still distribute steel from the site, although it is now stored indoors.

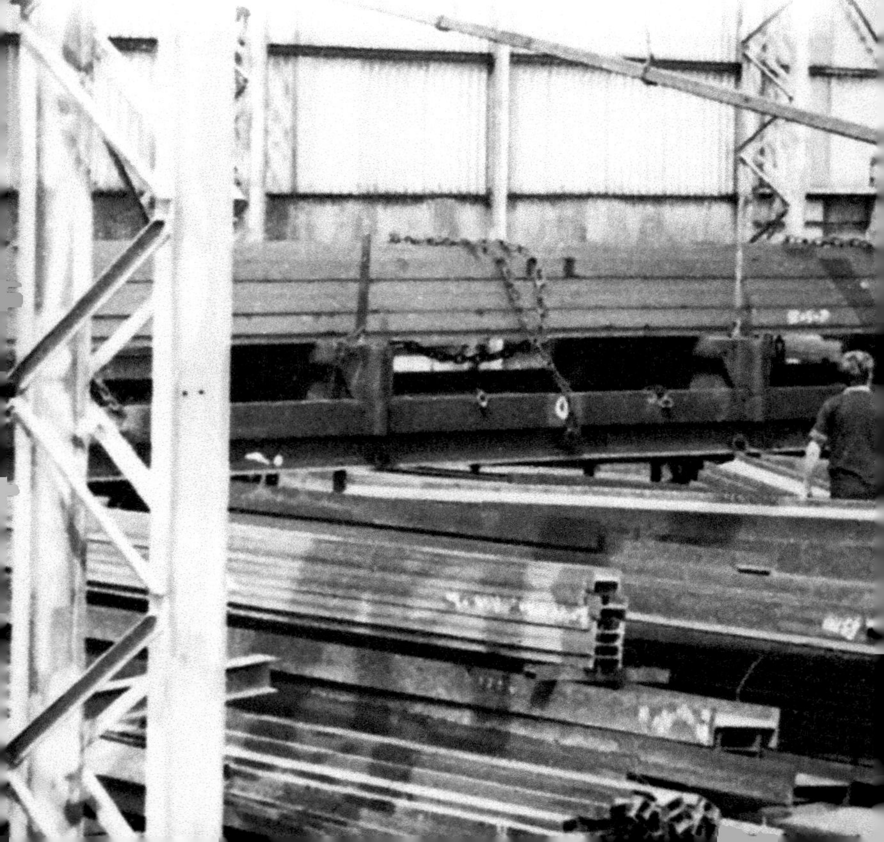

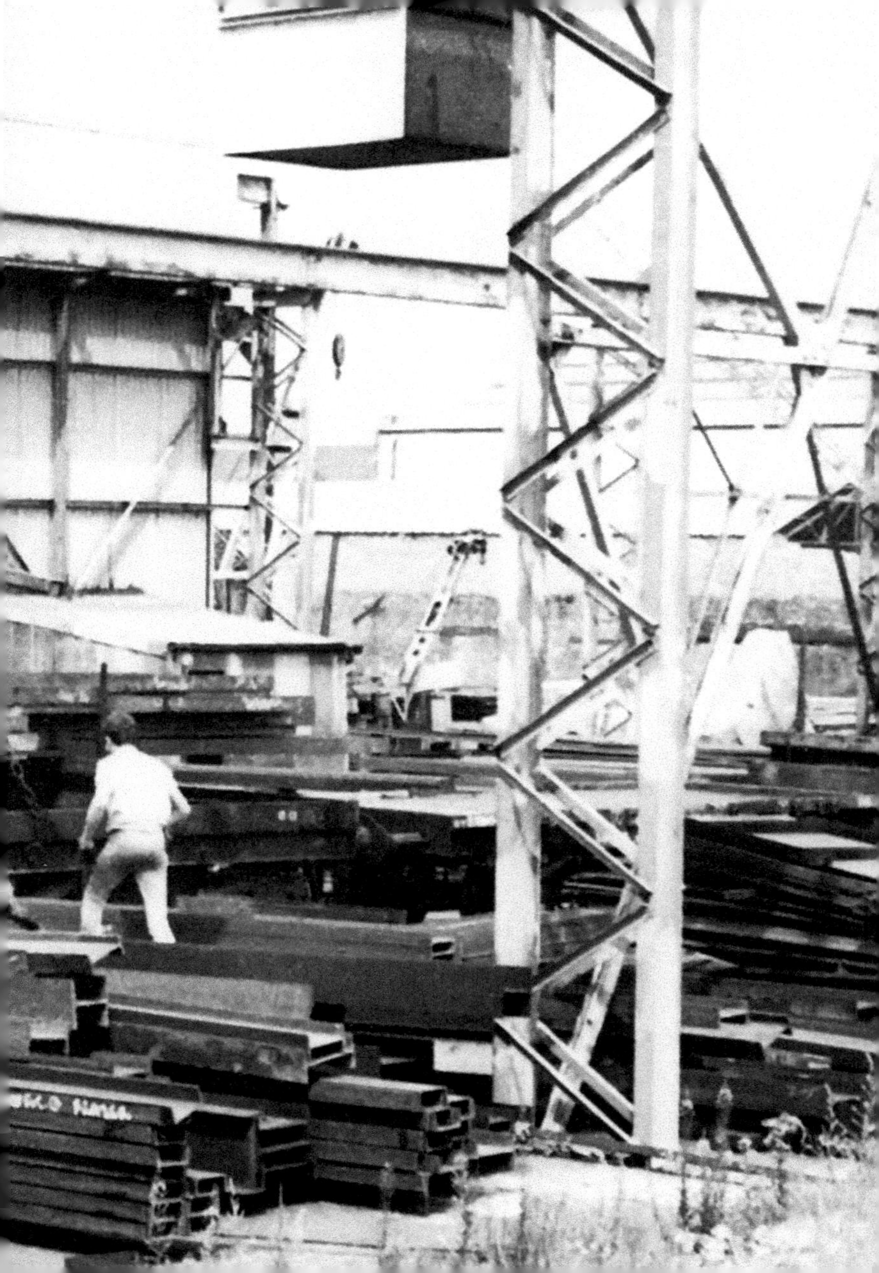

21. ST ALOYSIUS, *c.* 1925

During the Reformation of the 1500s, recusant Catholicism in Hebburn is first recorded when the Hodgson family hid priests at Hebburn Hall. Three centuries later a large immigrant workforce, many of them Irish Catholics, led to the provision of such a large building as St Aloysius. The French-style church is pictured here from Bell Street, with the old school buildings behind. A parish hall now stands alongside and a new Catholic school has been built further down Argyle Street.

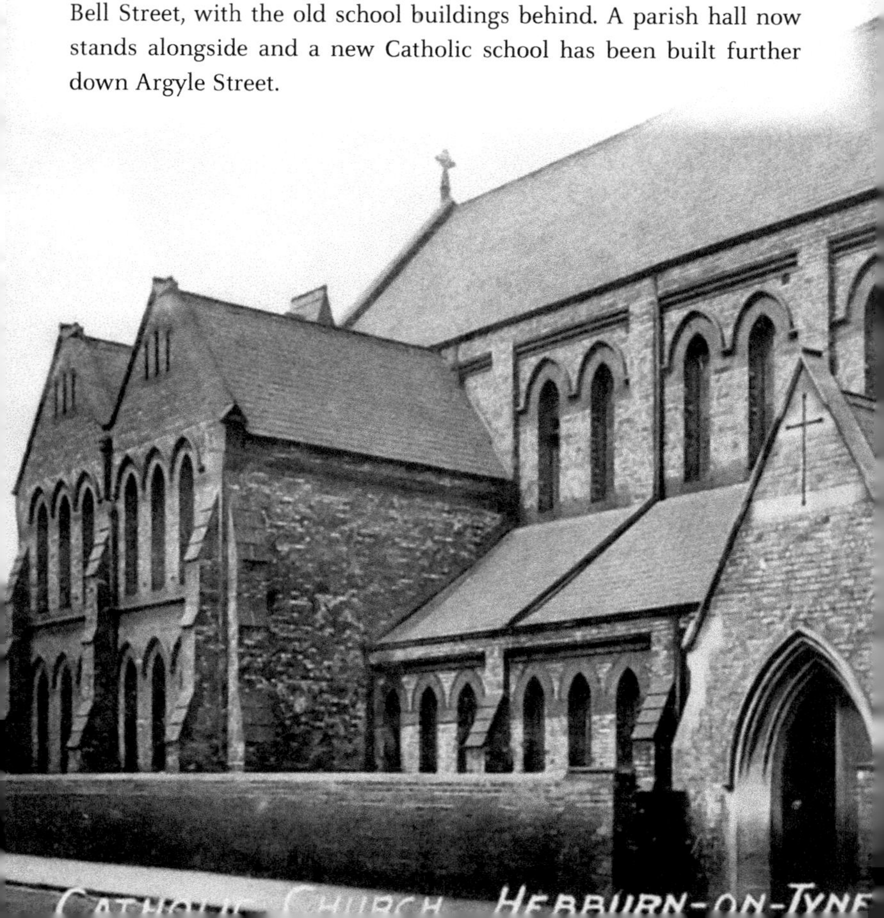

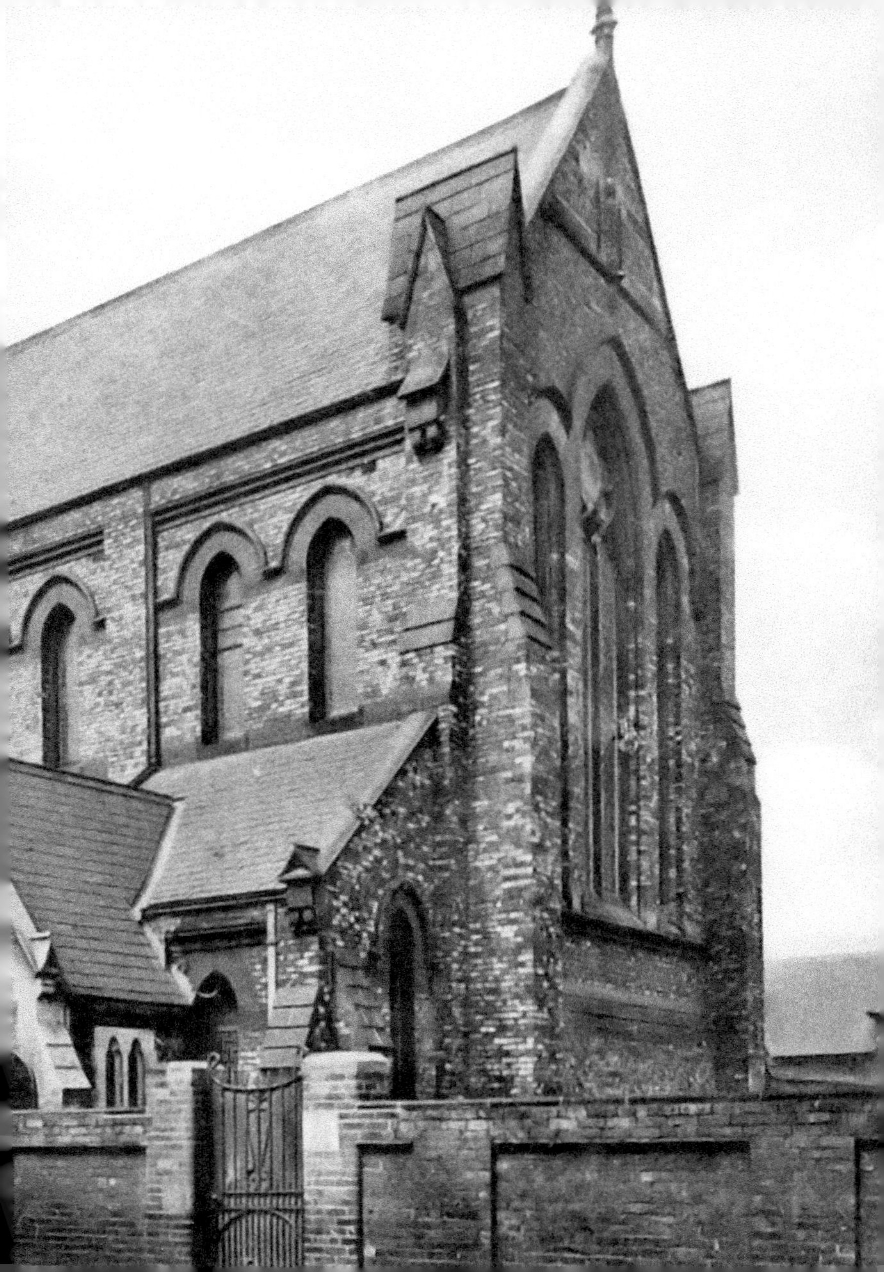

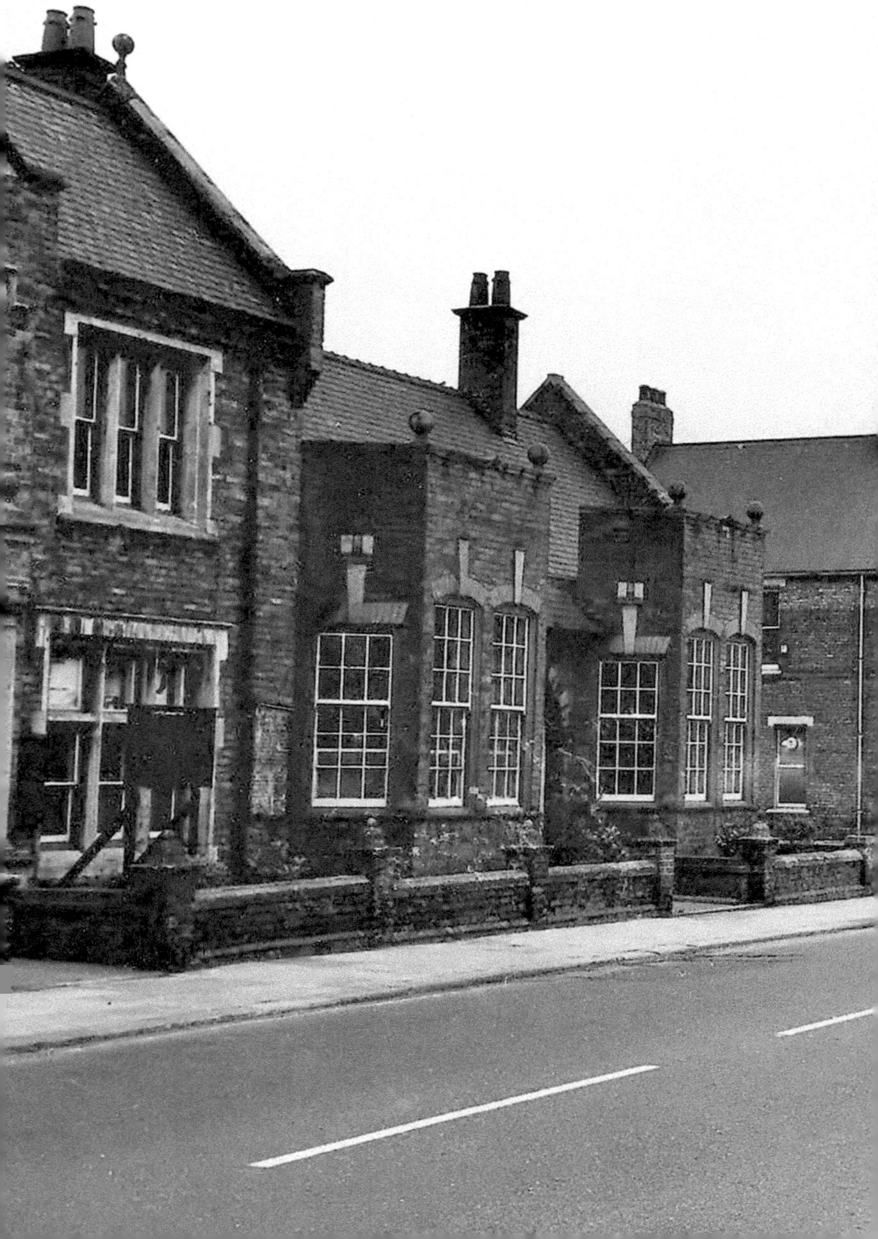

22. ARGYLE STREET POLICE STATION, c. 1970

Demolition of Argyle Street was underway when this photograph was taken. The old council chambers further down the street are waste ground and the fine police station buildings (far left) are only a few years away from demolition. Hebburn's police force experienced rowdy times in the early years. Opened in 1876, the police station survived an 1887 attempt to blow it up. Its ultra-modern but less eye-catching successor began operations on Victoria Road East in 1977.

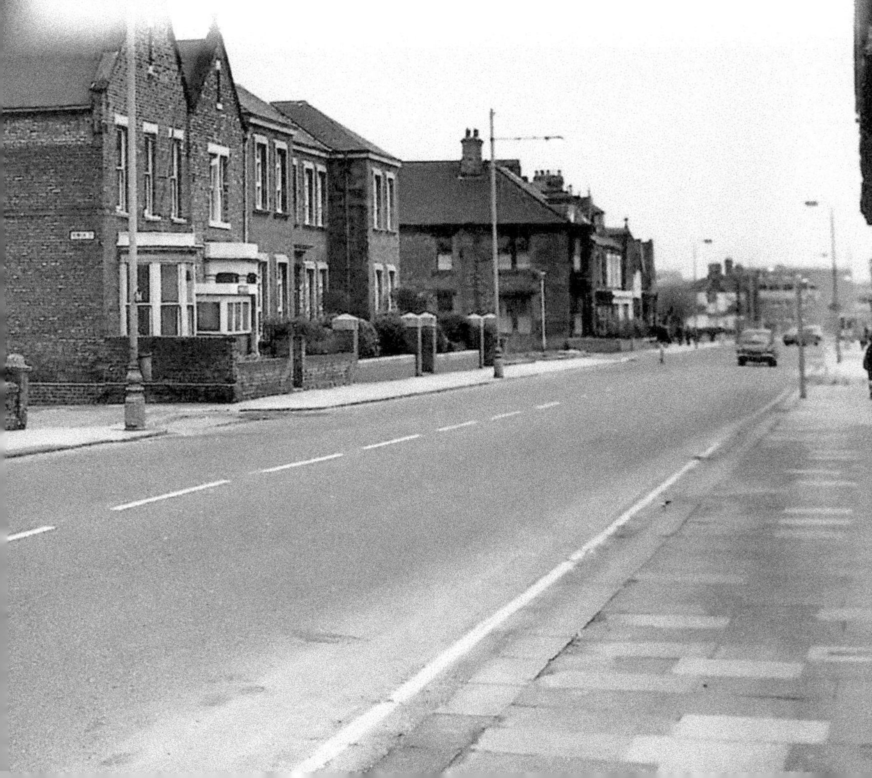

ELECTRIC POWER STATION

23. POWER STATION, *c.* 1900

Long before the National Grid, it was proposed to illuminate parts of Hebburn with cables from Leslie's shipyard. But it was not until after 1903 that gas lighting was supplemented by electricity from the Northern Counties Supply Company, which ran Hebburn's power station until superseded by larger Tyneside generators. In the 1930s its location beside the railway became Hebburn's social service centre, better known as the Power House. Clear views across the tracks have become obstructed but the area, now a substation, once again bristles with electrical equipment.

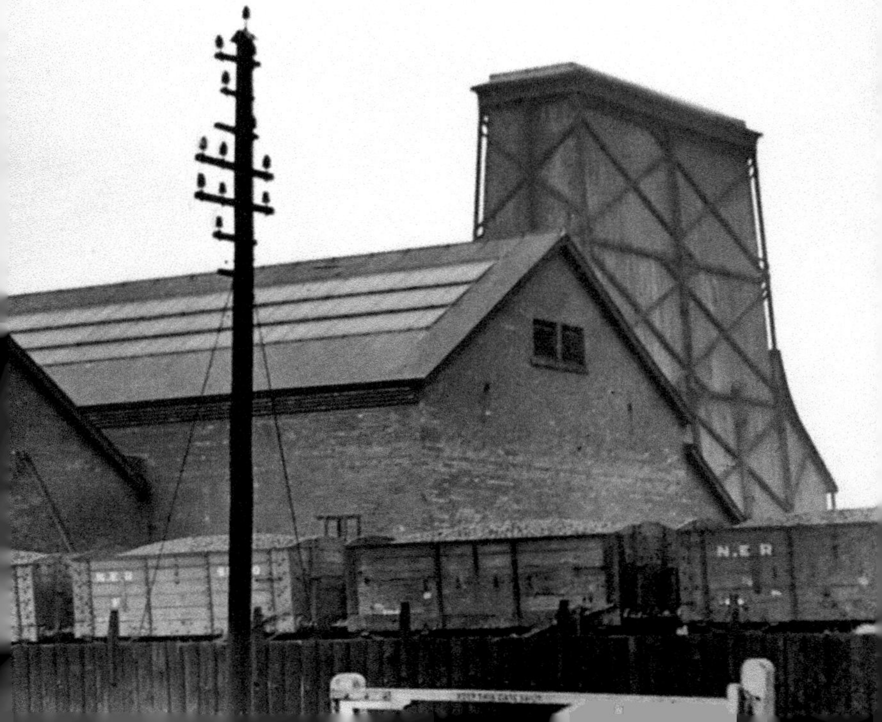

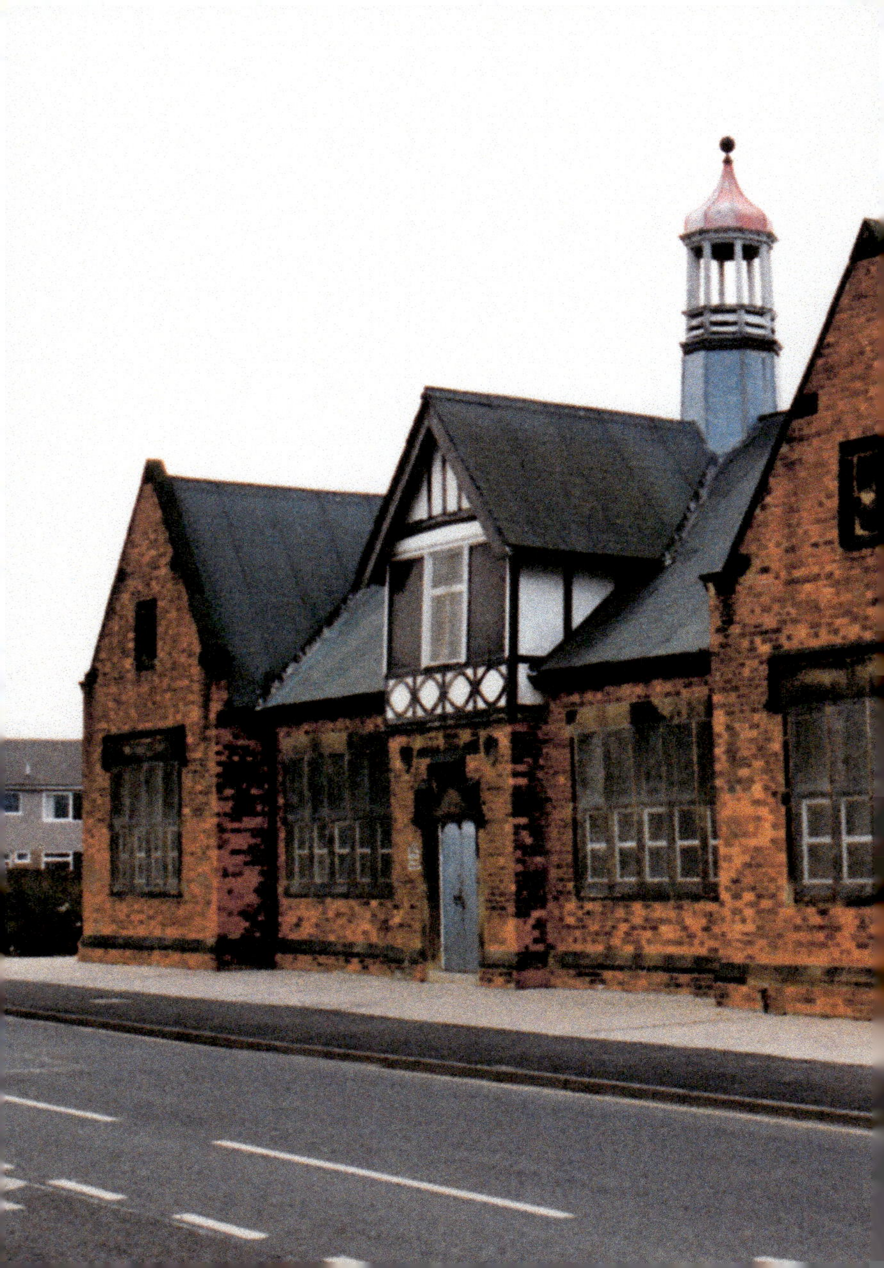

24. HEDLEY SUNDAY SCHOOL, ARGYLE STREET, *c.* 1995

Paid for by public subscription, this Sunday school was opened next to St Cuthbert's church on Easter Monday 1882. Shortly afterwards the Tudor-style building was named in memory of William Hedley, first vicar of St Cuthbert's who died at the age of just thirty-six. As well as being a schoolroom, the Hedley School building has found a variety of social purposes. During the Second World War it sheltered bomb victims, and it has recently been repaired and extended for even wider communal use.

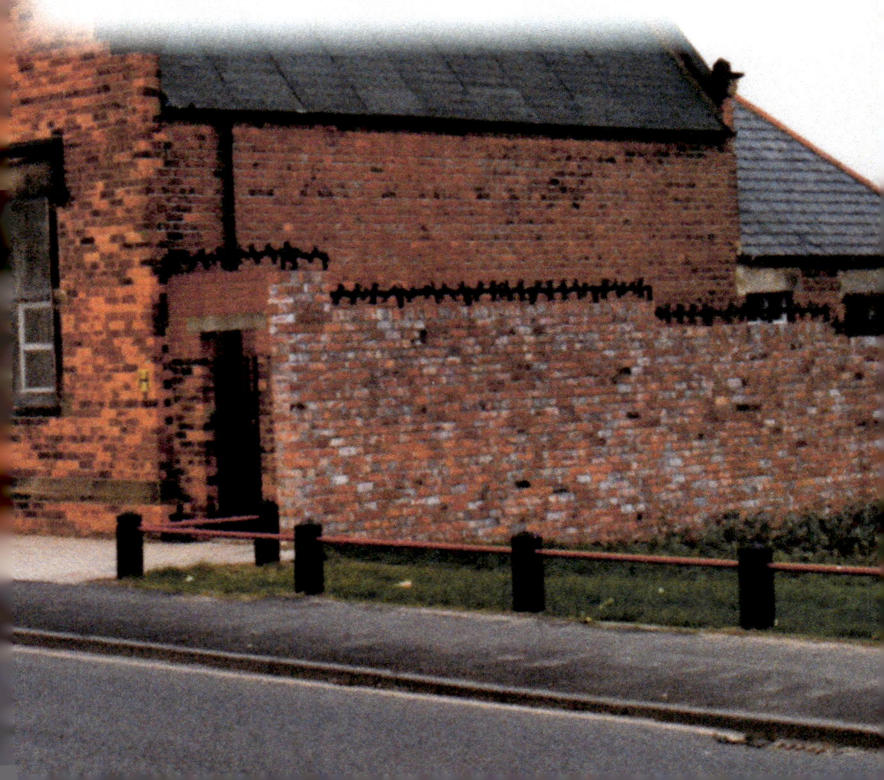

25. CARR STREET, EARLY 1900s

Named after Ralph Carr, inheritor of the Ellison estates in 1870, Carr Street was one of Hebburn Quay's busiest thoroughfares. Most of the children pictured above appear to be well dressed and shod but a barefoot boy strolls past No. 19 Carr Street – ironically Alfred Tyler's boot and shoe shop. The chimney in the distant murk belongs to 'C' pit, but nothing of it or Carr Street now survives to obstruct the view of St Andrew's church and institute.

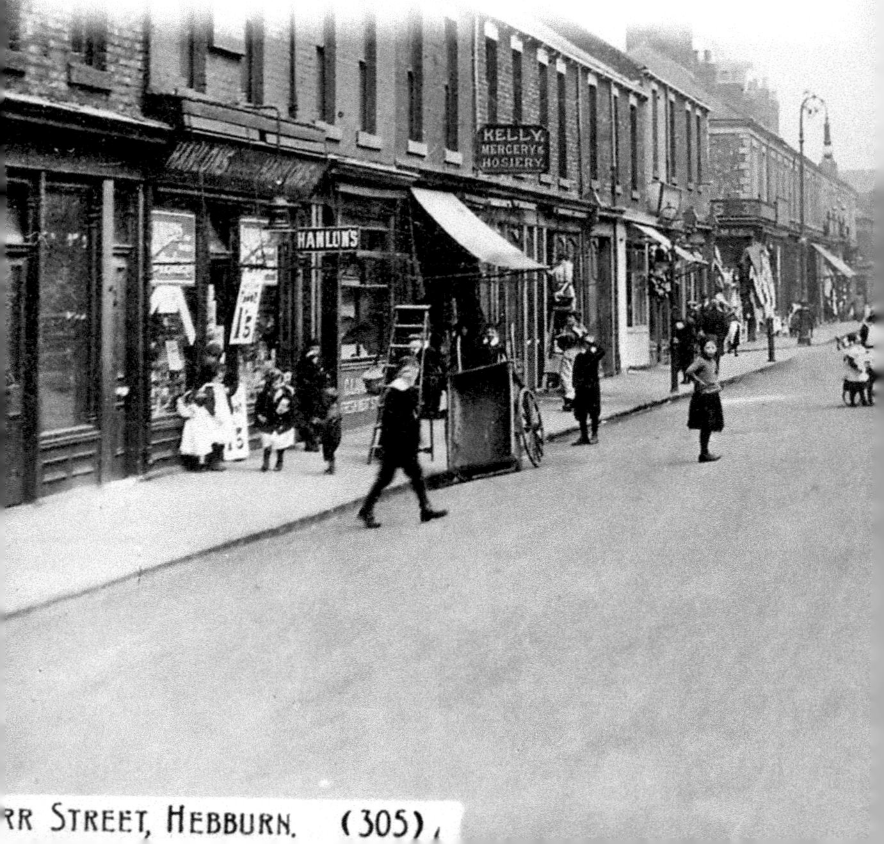

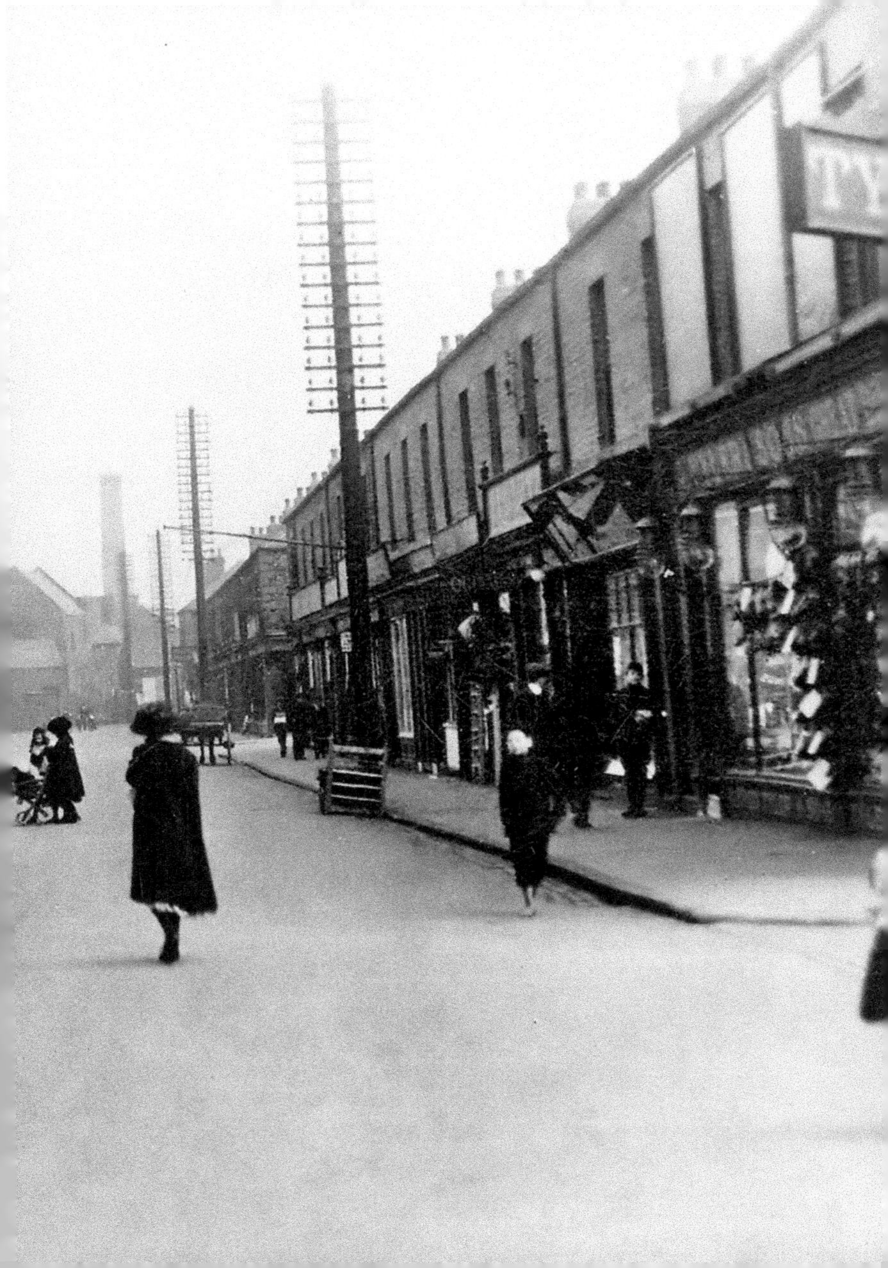

26. STUBBS' LANDING, HEBBURN QUAY, 1911

Charlie 'Sculler' Stubbs proudly surveys his domain at Hebburn Quay. He hailed from generations of scullermen – watermen who rowed their fares back and forth across the Tyne. A small boat can be glimpsed on his left, and behind him are the Ballast Hill and the Tyne View buildings erected for the Tennant Chemical Company. In the 1970s, 75 acres of derelict riverside were landscaped to create Hebburn Marina, recently improved with a new walkway, lighting and decorative guard rails.

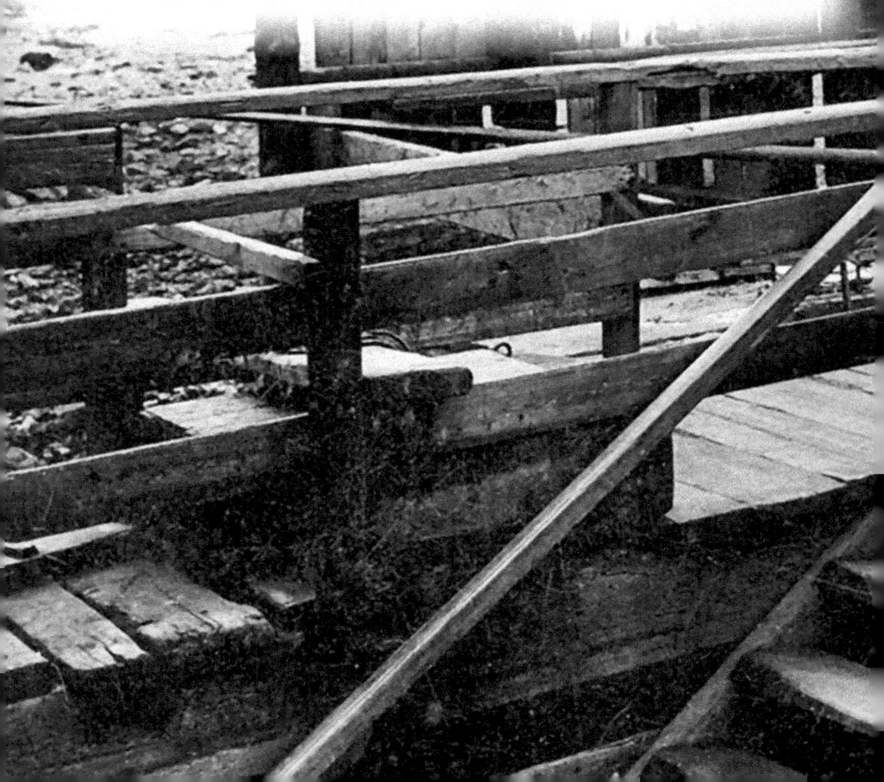

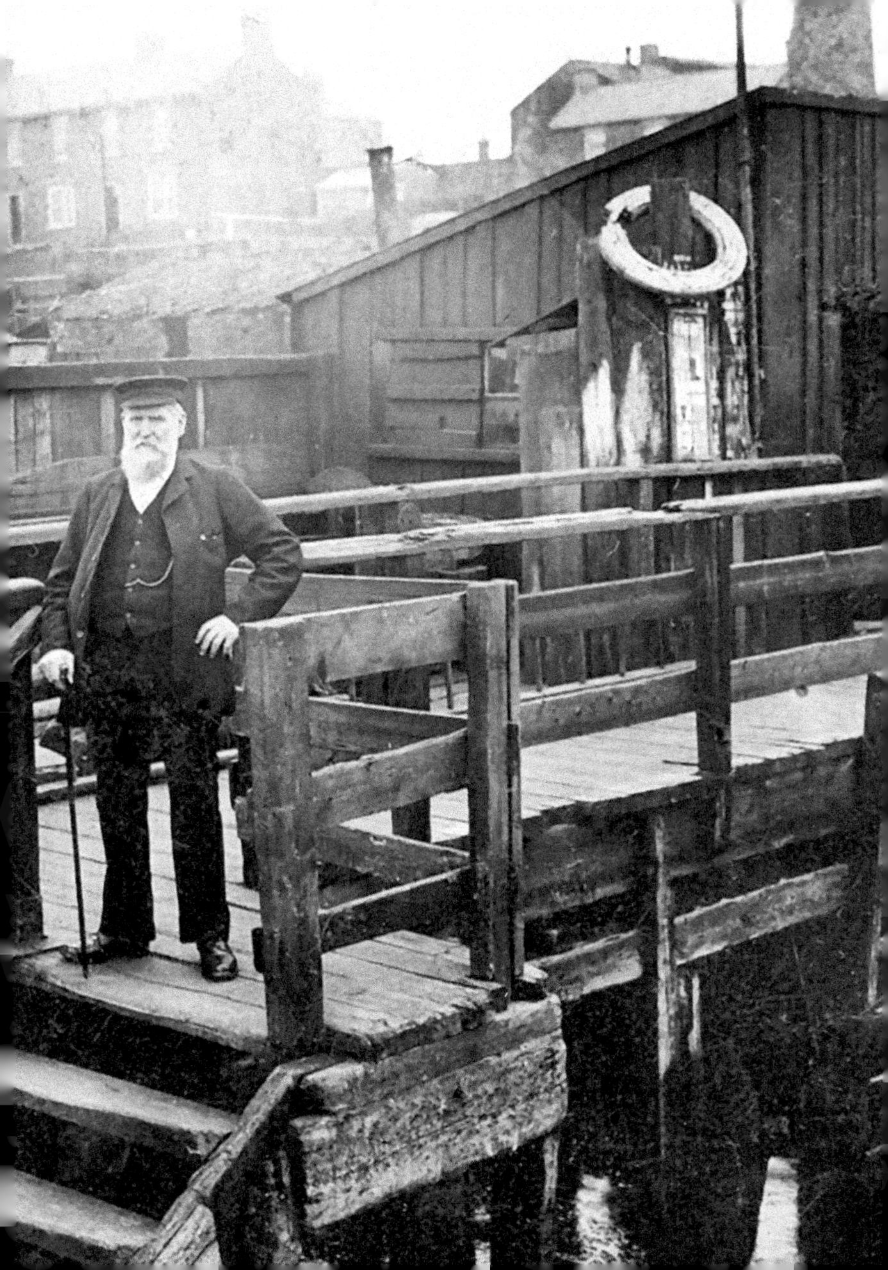

27. THE BALLAST HILL, 1964

Hebburn's Ballast Hill was a major riverside vantage point. This large artificial mound – one of many on Tyneside – was a centuries-old accumulation of mostly sand and gravel, used to stabilise sailing ships before replenishment with outgoing cargo (usually coal). Although the practice ended when steam vessels began to use water ballast in the mid-nineteenth century the hill was not fully removed until the 1970s. Fine cross-river views can still be had from many of the houses now on the site.

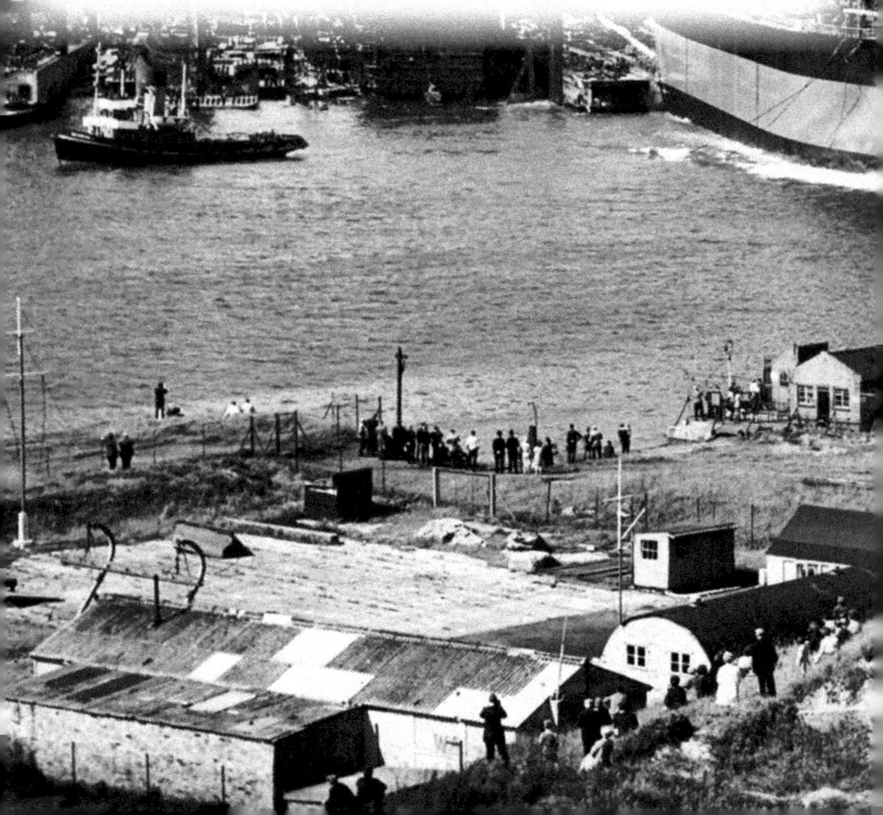

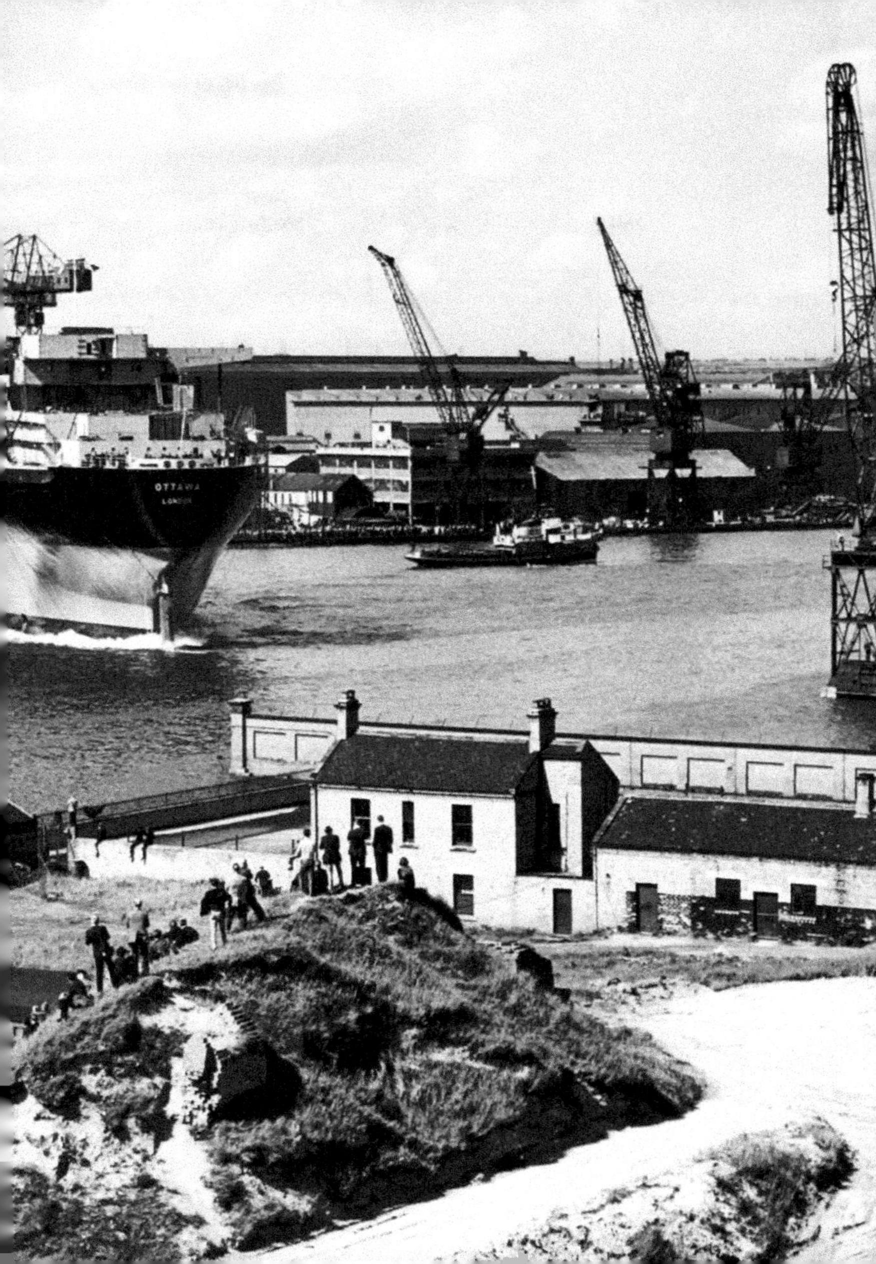
OTTAWA

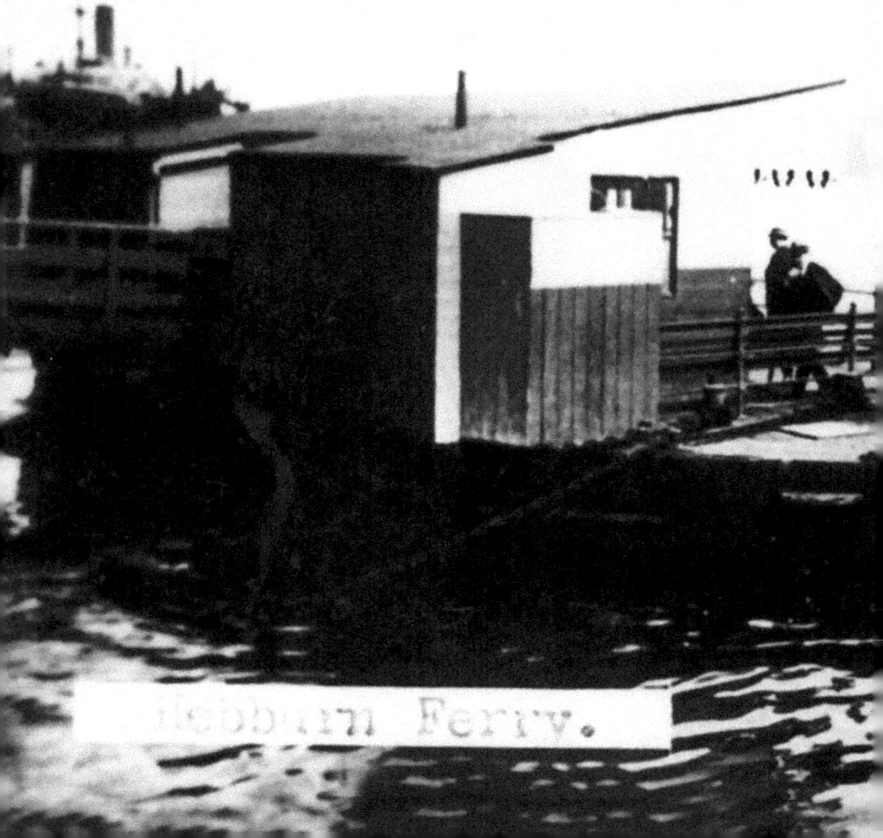
Hebburn Ferry.

28. HEBBURN FERRY, *c.* 1920

The first regular ferry service was established by Andrew Leslie in 1854. By the early twentieth century four steamboats shuttled between Hebburn, Wallsend and Walker. From 1939 Mid-Tyne Ferries introduced newer vessels, which at their peak carried over a million passengers annually. Tyneside's industrial decline had inevitable consequences, however, and Hebburn's last ferry sailed in 1986. Anglers have replaced hurrying crowds of shipyard and factory workers on today's Hebburn quayside.

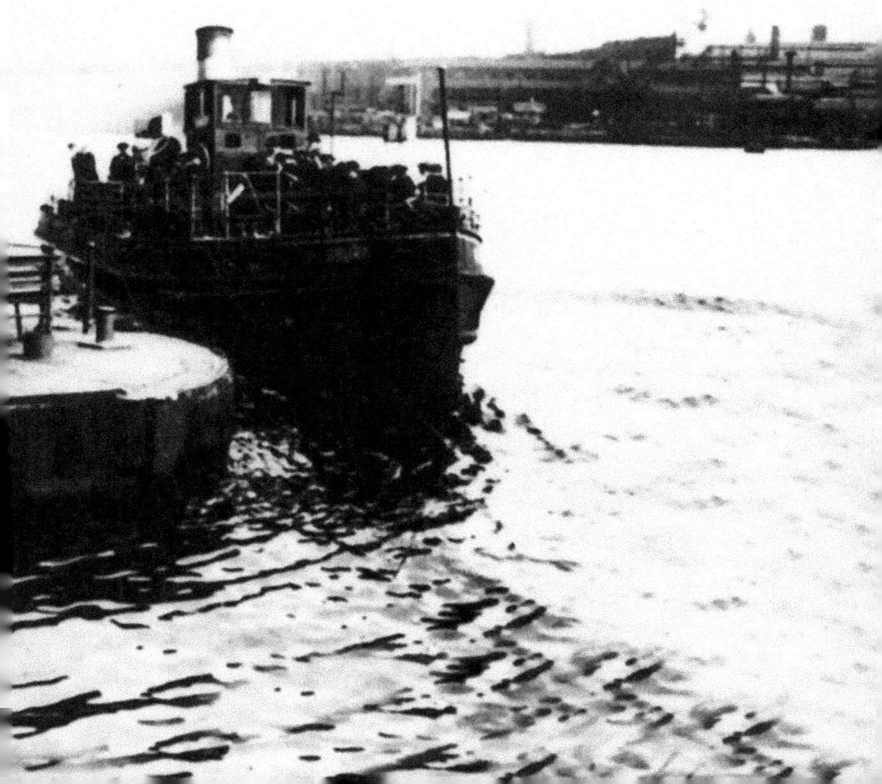

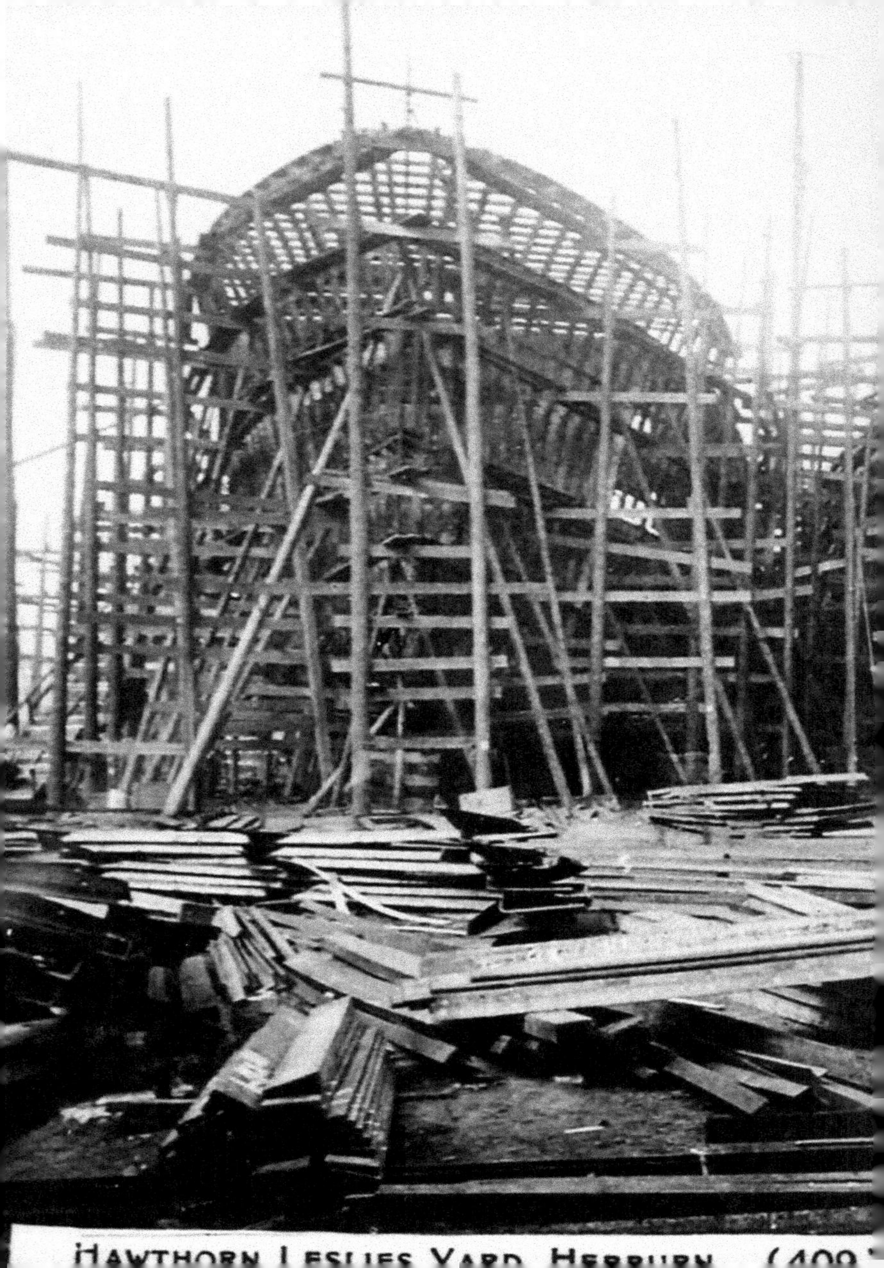
HAWTHORN LESLIES YARD, HEBBURN. (409)

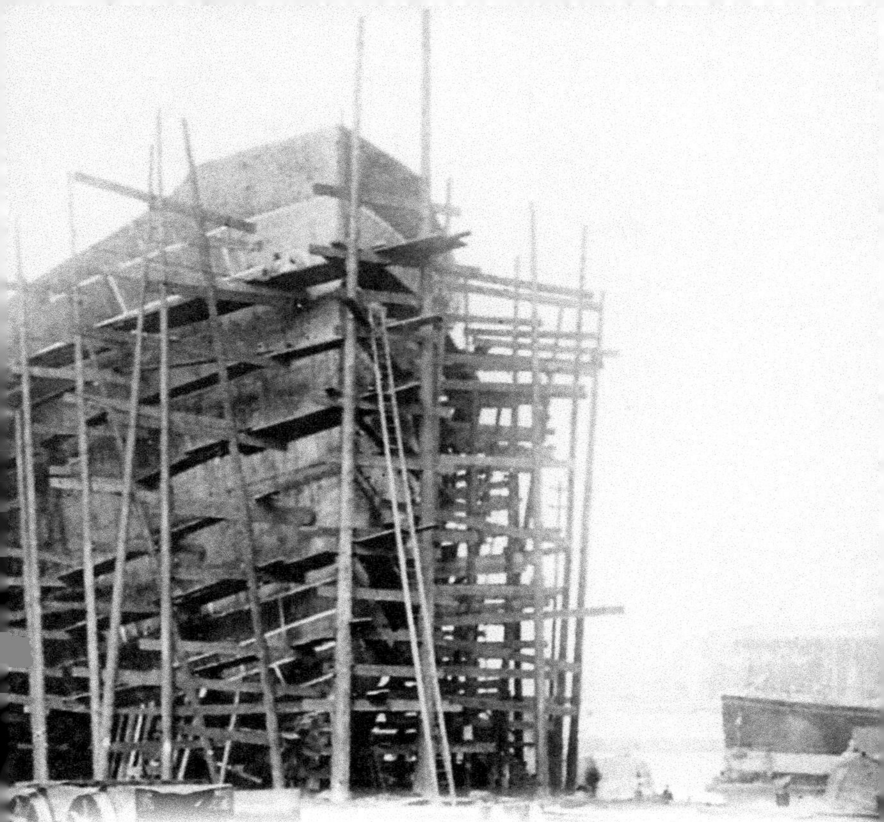

29. LESLIE'S SHIPBUILDERS, *c.* 1900

Andrew Leslie turned a sand-banked location into a flourishing business. Auxiliary steam sailing craft Clarendon was the first vessel to be launched at Hebburn in 1854, followed over the years by more than 700 ships. After closure in 1982, the historic shipyard was used as a training centre, and now ship repairers A. & P. Tyne occupy parts of it. The company has helped keep Hebburn's maritime heritage afloat, though the grass grows over Hawthorn Leslie's old slipways.

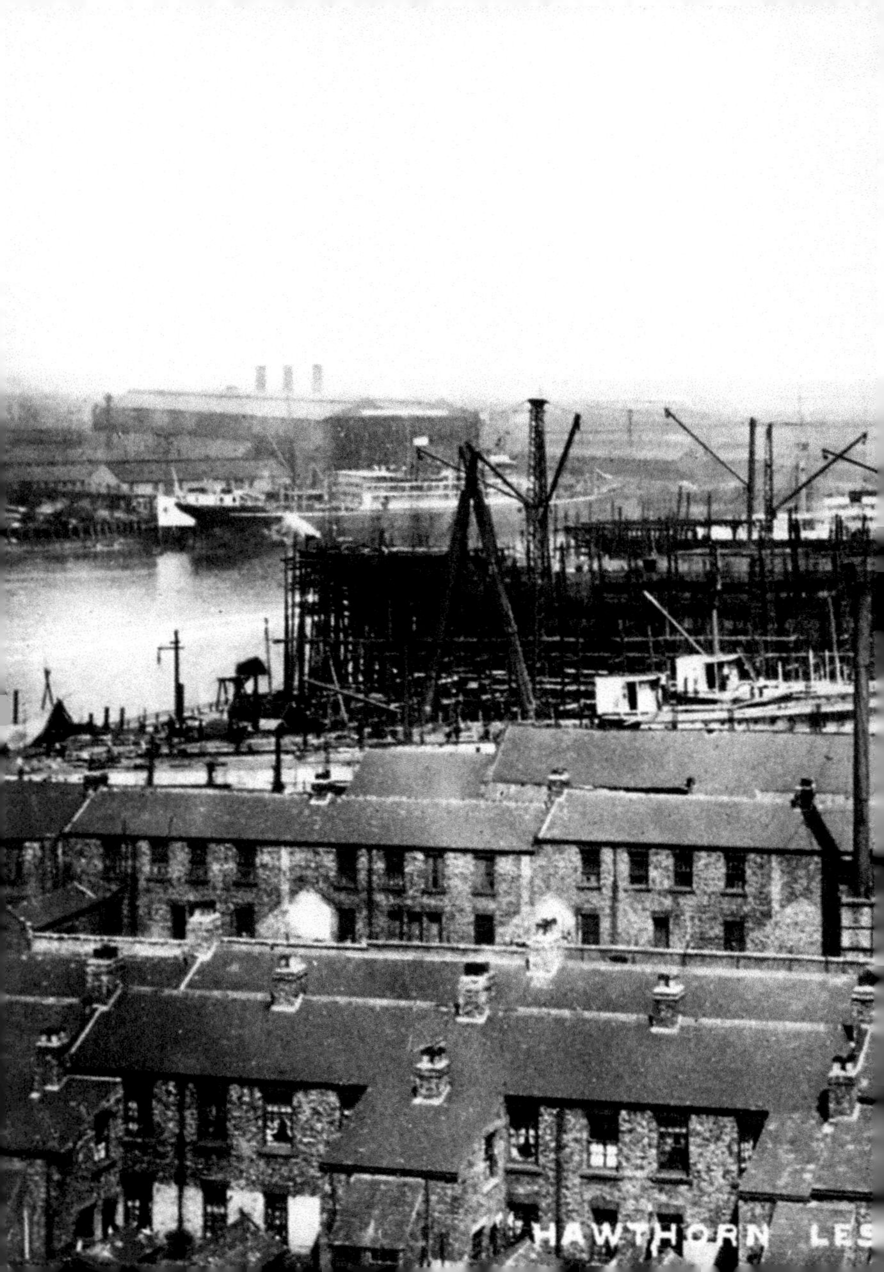
HAWTHORN LES

30. HAWTHORN LESLIE'S SHIPYARD, 1916/17

After Andrew Leslie's retirement in 1886, his Ellison Street business amalgamated with Newcastle engineers R. W. Hawthorn and continued to build and repair ships in the Hebburn yard. Its slipways and 1866 dry dock are shown here beyond the foreground rooftops of Bonaccord Street. This was the heart of Hebburn's shipbuilding community, where most property was built and rented out by the shipyard founder. Now the old 'Leslie's Houses' have been replaced by a new Hebburn 'Village' and only a few sad fragments remain of the great enterprise that Leslie began.

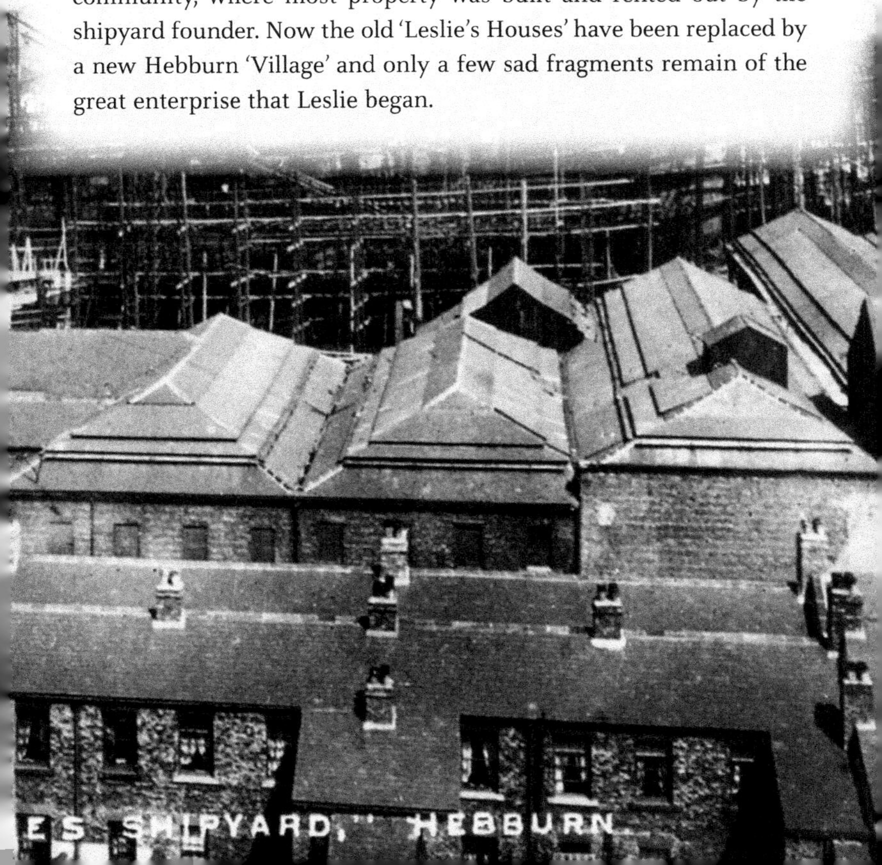

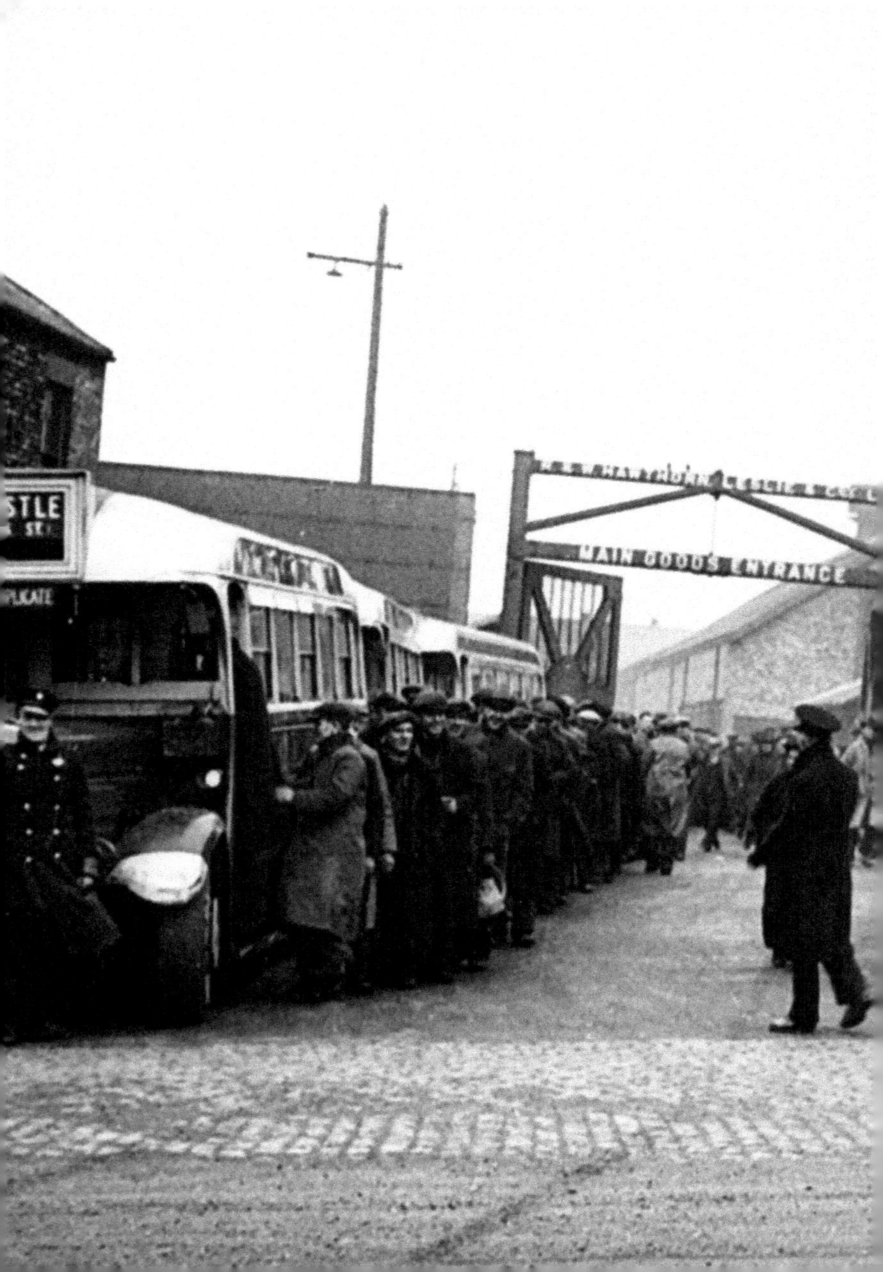
MAIN GOODS ENTRANCE

31. ST ANDREW'S STREET, 1950s

Hawthorn Leslie's experienced relative prosperity in the post-war years. Its workforce of around 2,000 was kept busy with a steady stream of orders, replacing wartime losses and then building oil tankers and cargo vessels for increasing world trade. The shipyard's independence ended in 1968 when it became part of Swan Hunter & Tyne Shipbuilders Ltd. The spot where workmen once filed onto buses at the shipyard's 'top gate' is now Jedmoor, part of the 1988 Hebburn Village housing development.

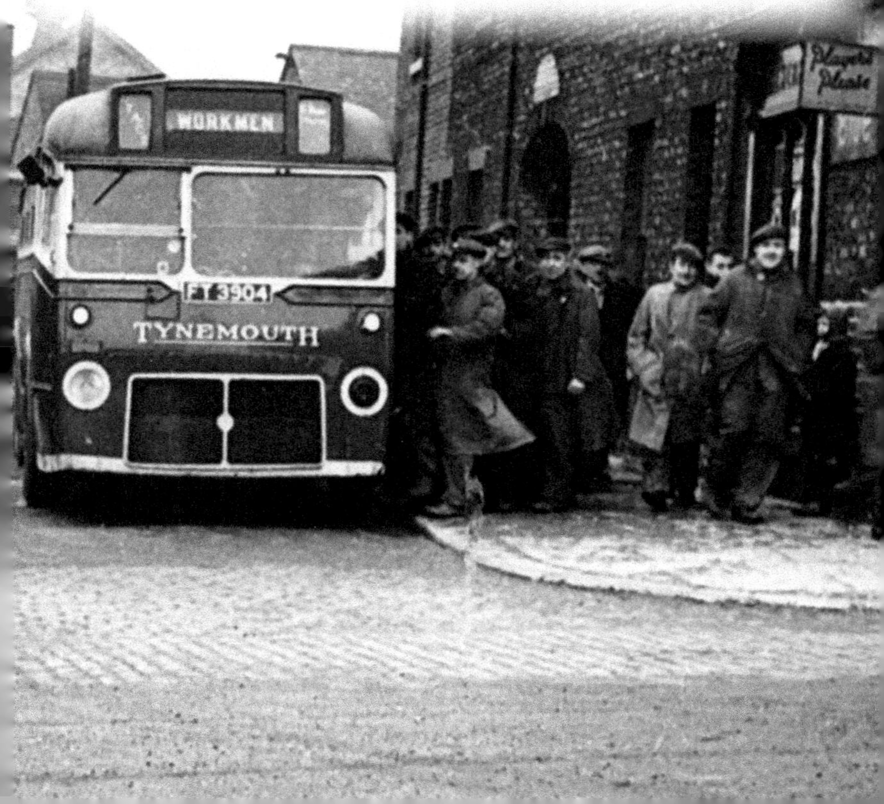

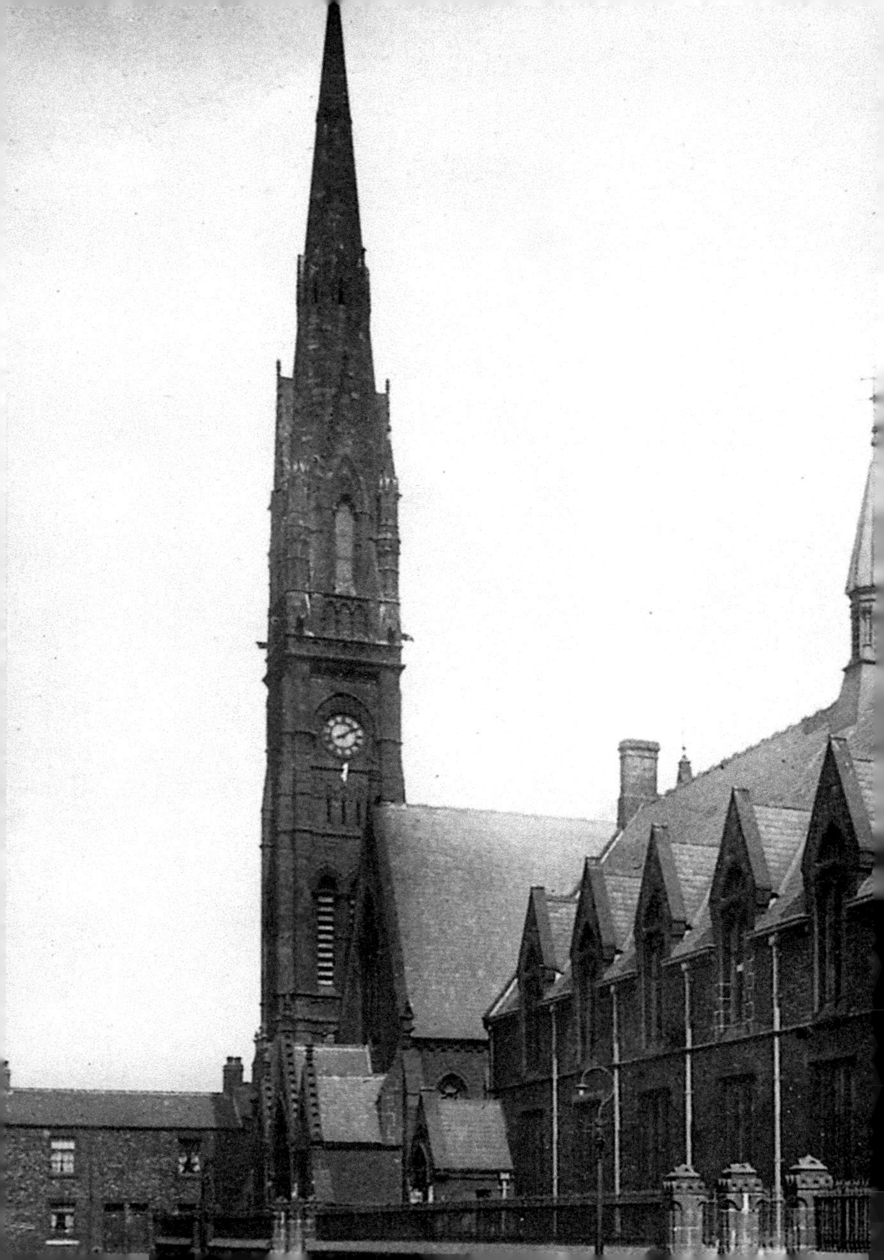

32. ST ANDREW'S INSTITUTE, 1918

Like many Victorian industrialists, Andrew Leslie encouraged the education of his workforce. He subsidised the building of a new Mechanics' Institute, comprising schoolhouse, lecture and assembly rooms, which opened on Church Street in January 1872. It went on to be a focus for the community and was restored in 1985. Seven years later it was purchased by the local council to house business units and is now used as a meditation centre.

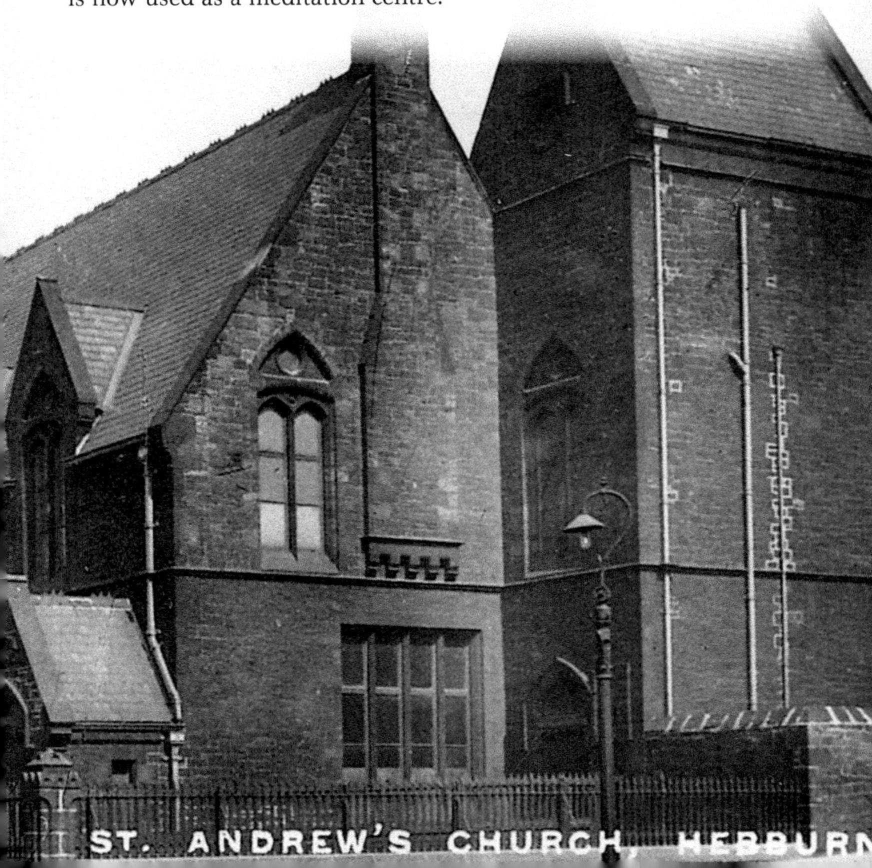

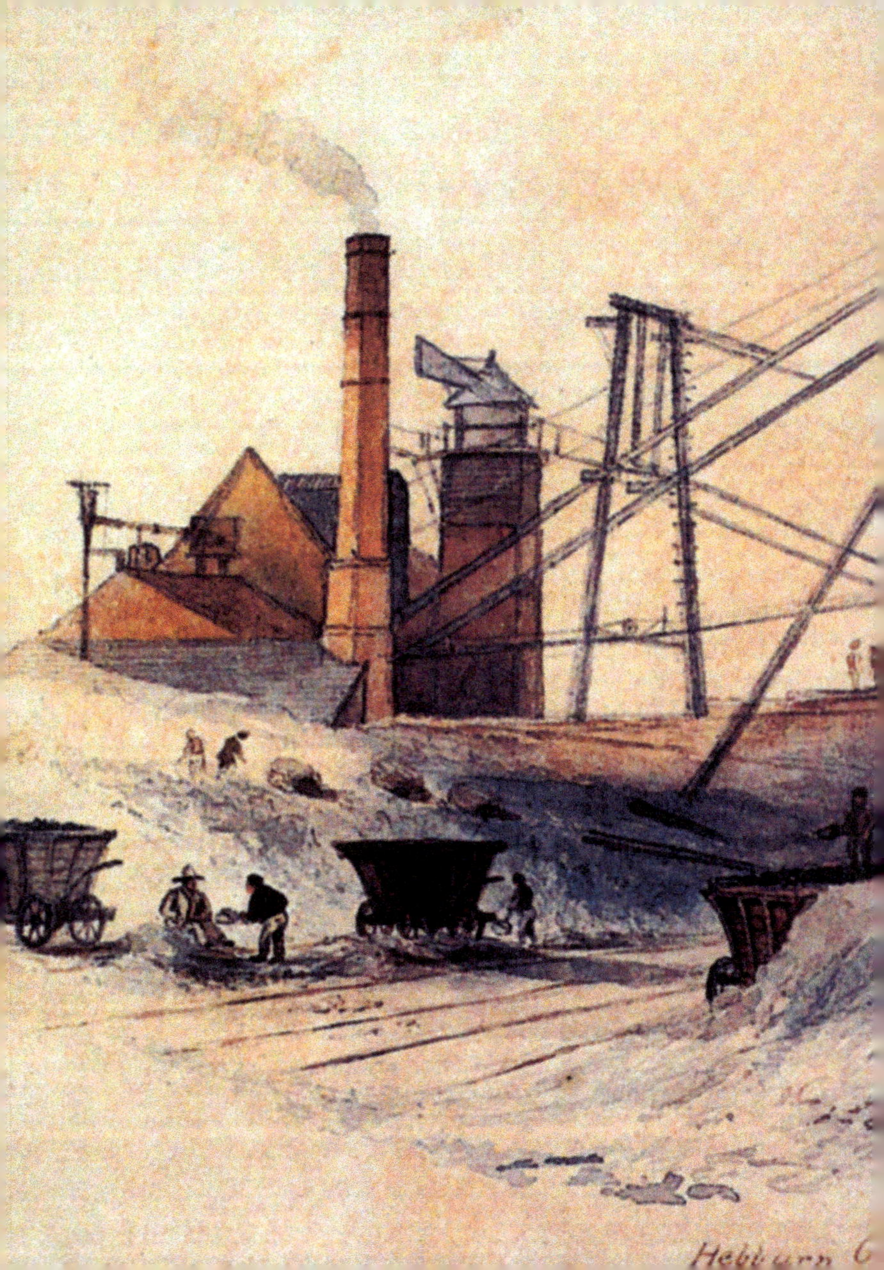
Hebburn C

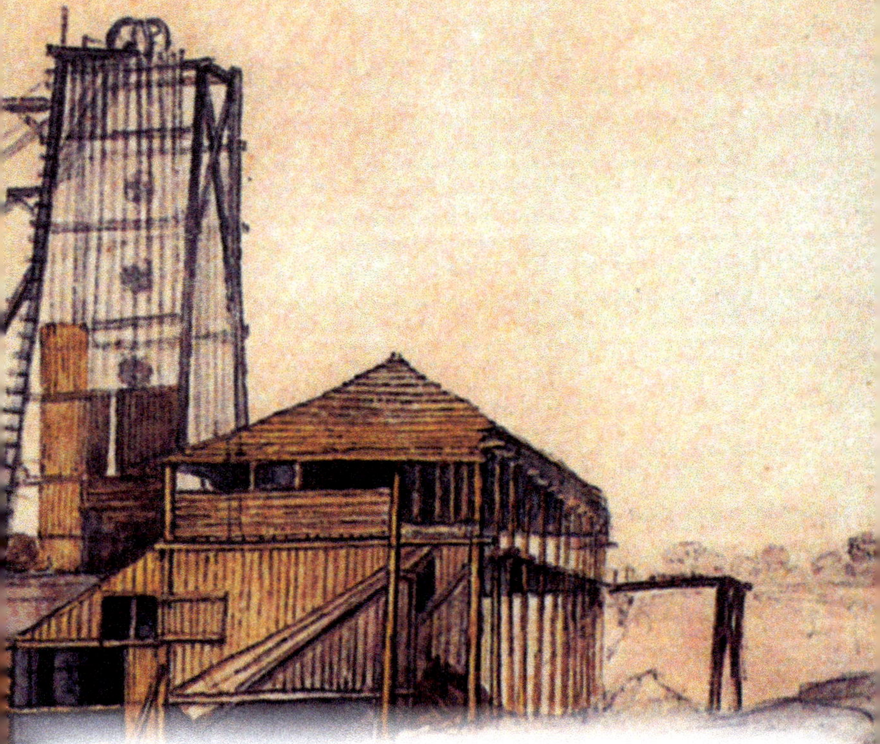

33. HEBBURN COLLIERY 'C' PIT, 1838

Hebburn's 'C' pit was sunk at the end of the eighteenth century on the riverside slope where houses are today at the top of Ellison Street. Thomas Hair's painting shows the colliery at full swing with the pit shaft and its head gear in the centre and a smoking engine chimney and vaned ventilator on the left. Coal is being shovelled into wagons or 'chaldrons' and what may be a wagonway appears indistinctly in the foreground.

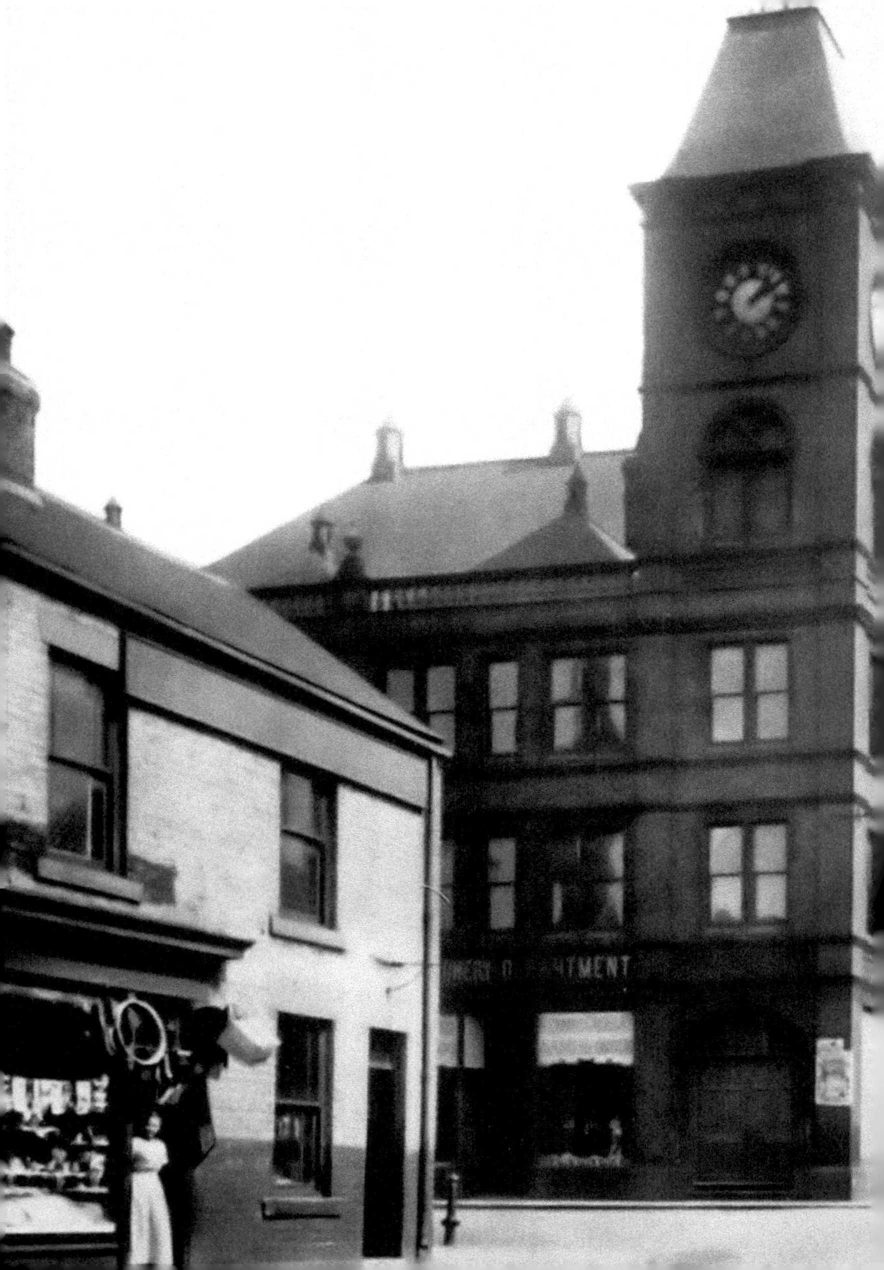

34. ALBERT STREET AND CO-OP BUILDINGS, *c.* 1910

Standing tall at the junction of Albert and Lyon Streets, the Co-op store was among the district's most impressive structures. Opened in June 1902 by local publican John S. Roy, the new building indicated the success of Hebburn's Co-operative movement; it had outgrown smaller premises on Lyon Street. With its upstairs assembly room, Hebburn's Store Hall became a popular shop and social venue. Of Edwardian Albert Street only the Albert Hotel (centre right, now Wardles) remains.

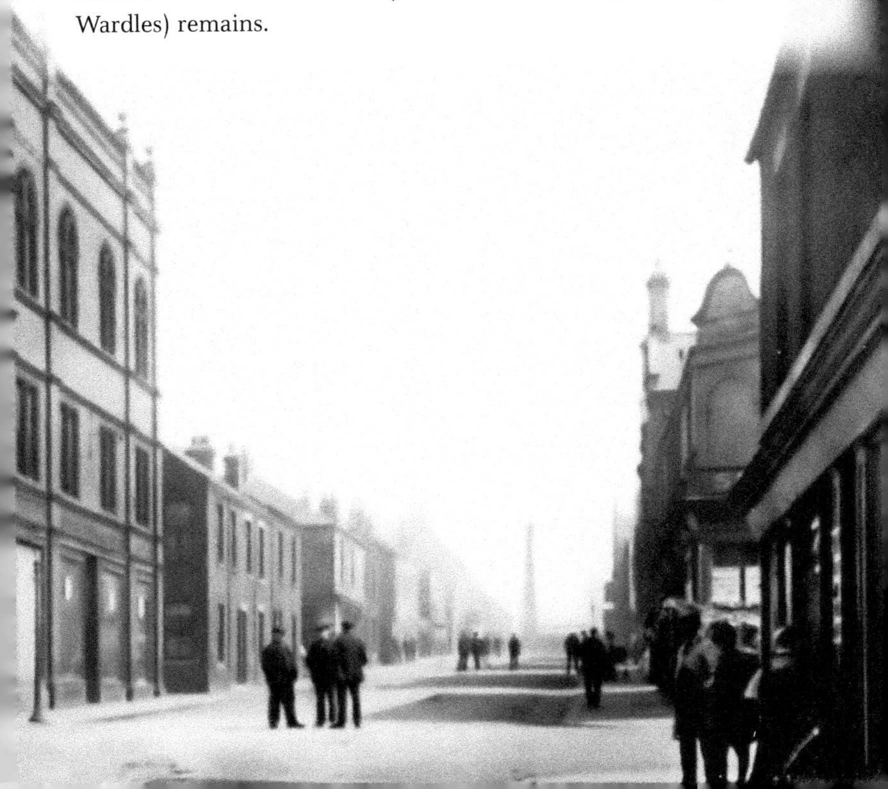

35. ELLISON STREET, *c.* 1911

Inquisitive townspeople stand and stare on the slope of Ellison Street at its junction with Lyon Street. Behind them are William Street and Cuthbert Street, part of an area of crowded terraces that were demolished from the late 1950s. They were replaced by a more spacious layout of modern housing and care homes, one of which is named after Ada Davies, a respected Hebburn councillor.

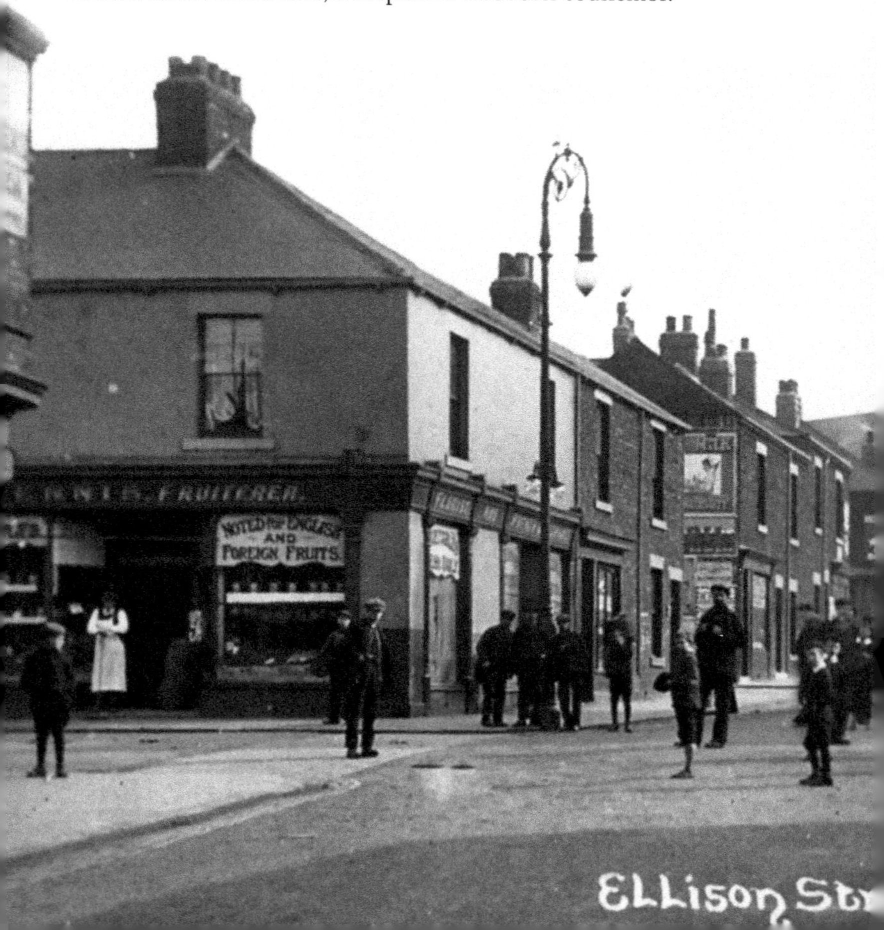

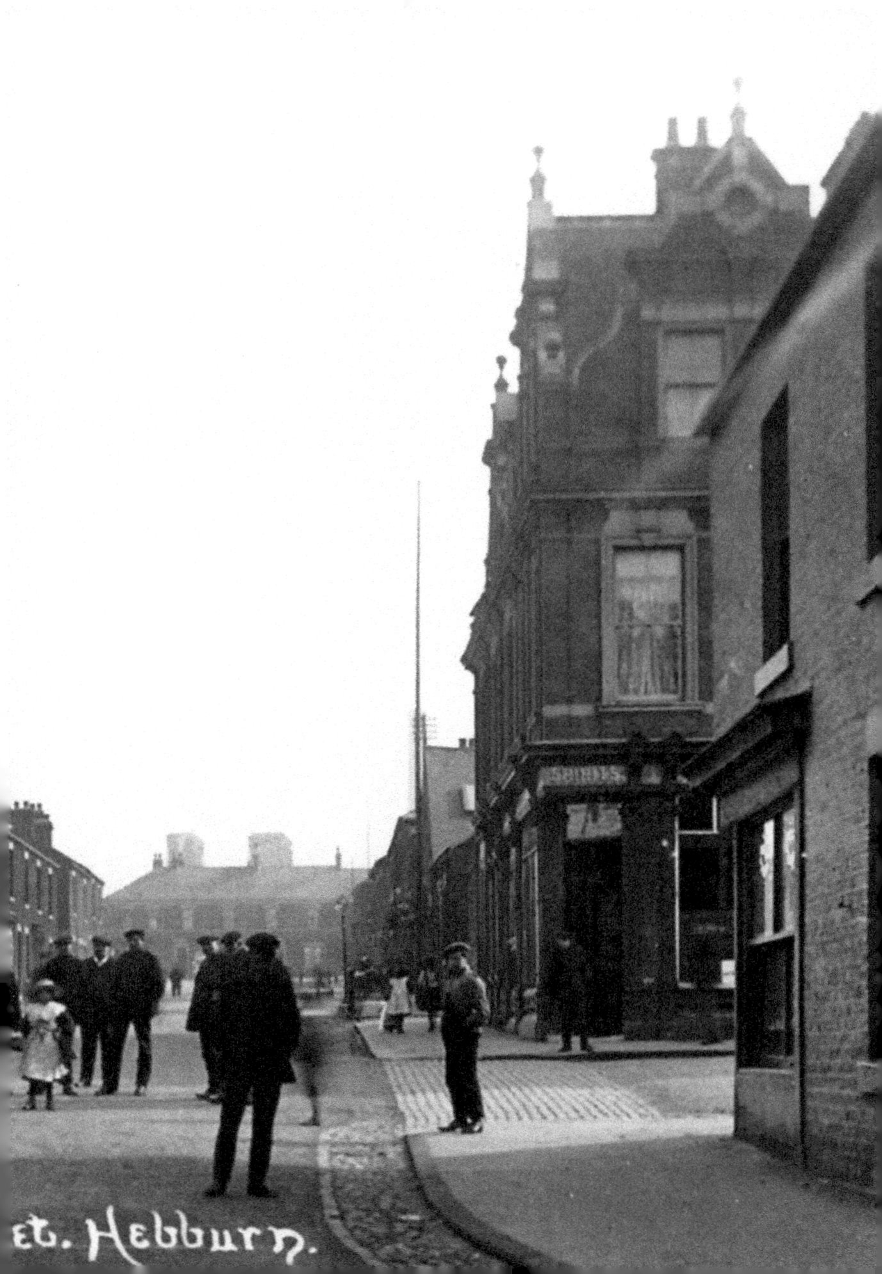
et. Hebburn.

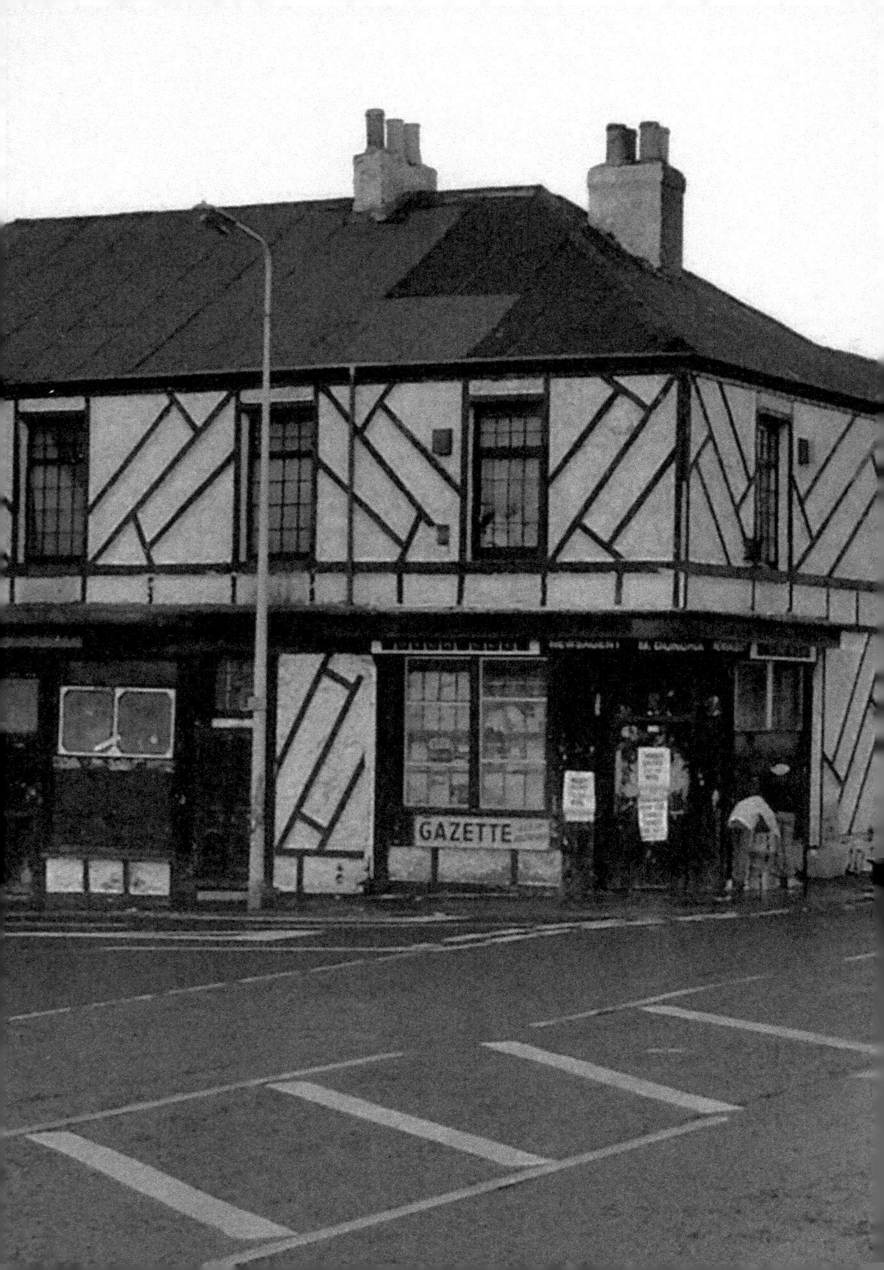
GAZETTE

36. JUNCTION OF ELLISON AND LYON STREETS, *c.* 1970

Donohue's corner shop lingered on after the Hebburn Quay house clearances of the 1960s and '70s. It had succeeded Hewison's, also a newsagent, and shared the corner site with a private local history museum and a florist. Michael Donohue remains a 'paperman', and before these curious buildings were finally demolished to make way for modern housing in 1994 he transferred his business to a much busier location in the town centre.

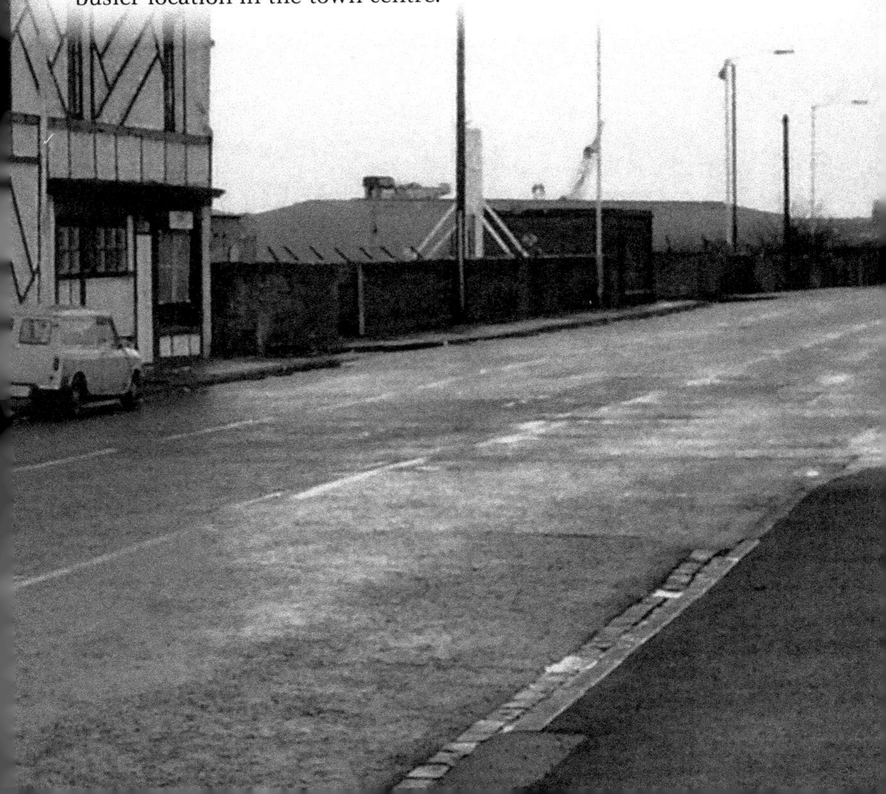

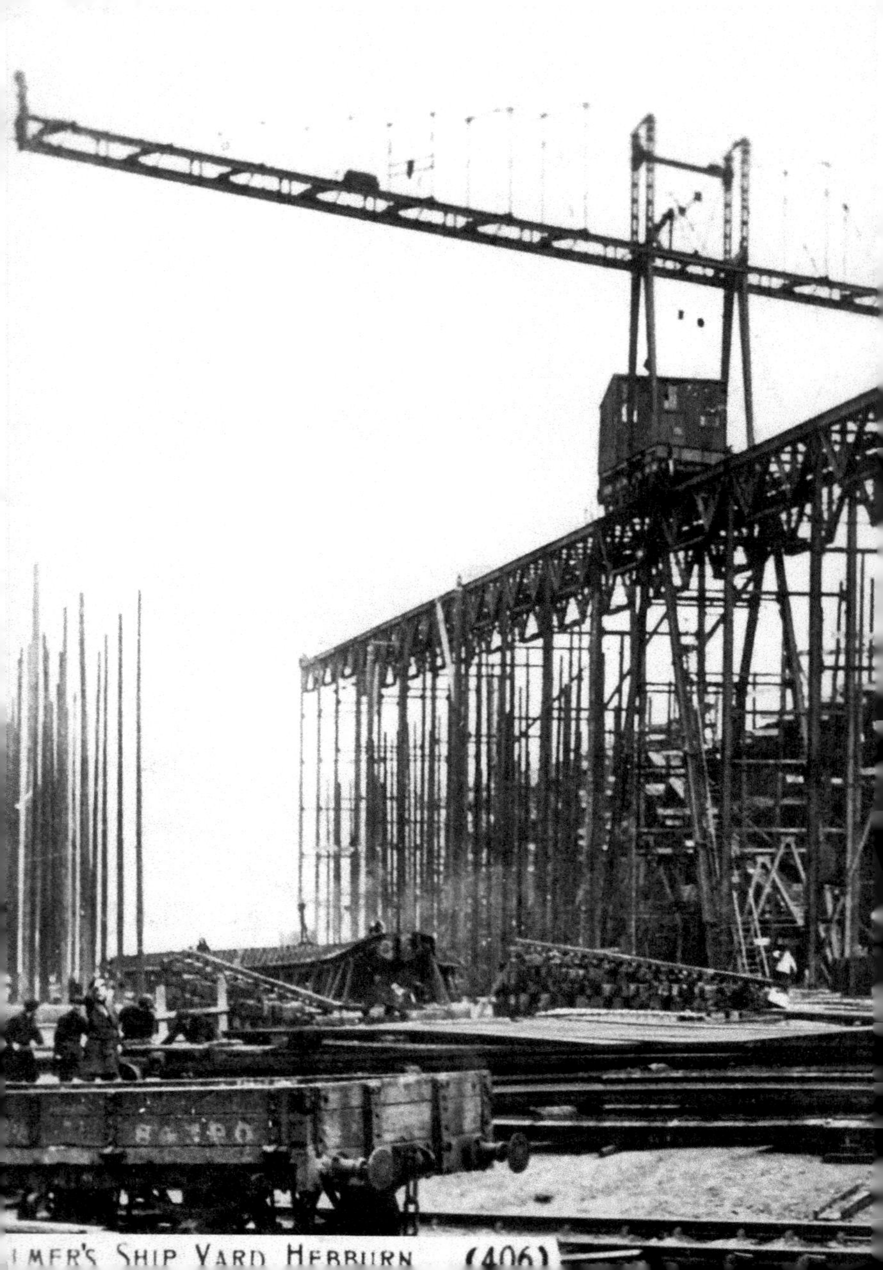
LMER'S SHIP YARD HEBBURN (406)

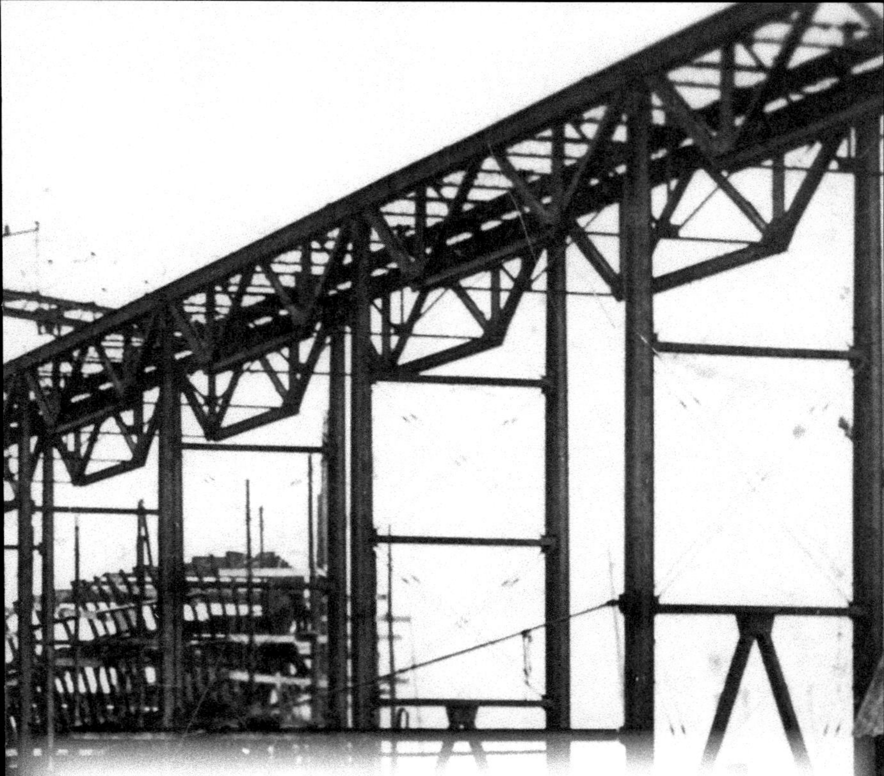

37. PALMER'S HEBBURN, *c.* 1915

Palmer's was another familiar Hebburn shipbuilding name. In 1912 the company acquired the yard adjacent to Hawthorn Leslie, formerly owned by Robert Stephenson, which contained the largest dry dock in the region. Shipbuilding ended there in 1931, but ship repair continued under the ownership of Vickers-Armstrong. An even larger dock was built in the 1960s and the Palmer's name survived until closure in 1970 with the loss of almost 1,000 jobs. A. & P. Tyne maintains something of the old Leslie & Palmer's tradition today, employing around 200 people.

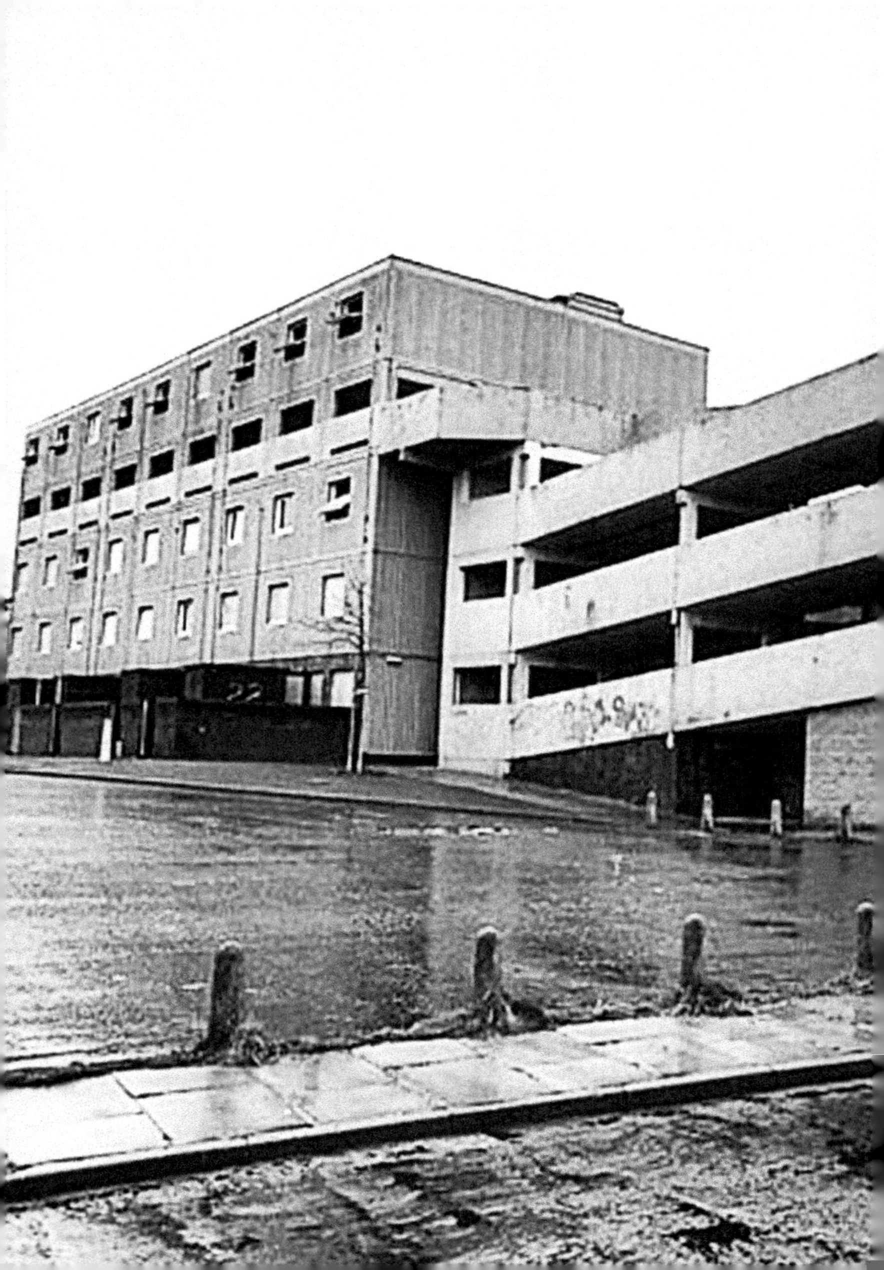
22

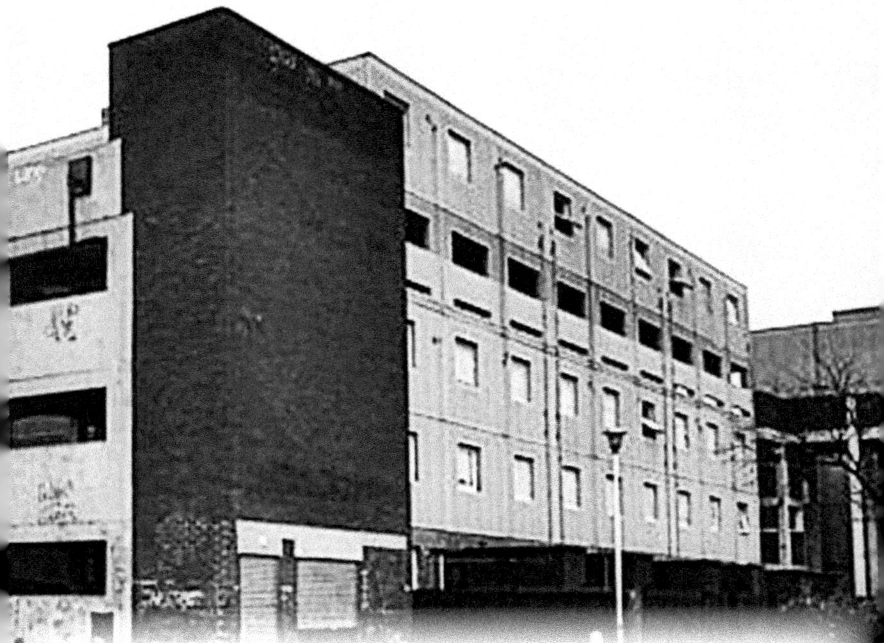

38. SCHOOL STREET FLATS, *c.* 1989

The School Street scheme failed to solve Hebburn's post-war housing shortage. The ambitious five-year plan was set to transform disused land between the old colliery and the quay. Building began in 1966, spreading out from the School Street site. Although initially well received, the flats were costly to maintain and their brutalist architecture became increasingly unpopular. They were flattened after hardly more than twenty years. Traditional terraced-style houses are now gradually taking their place.

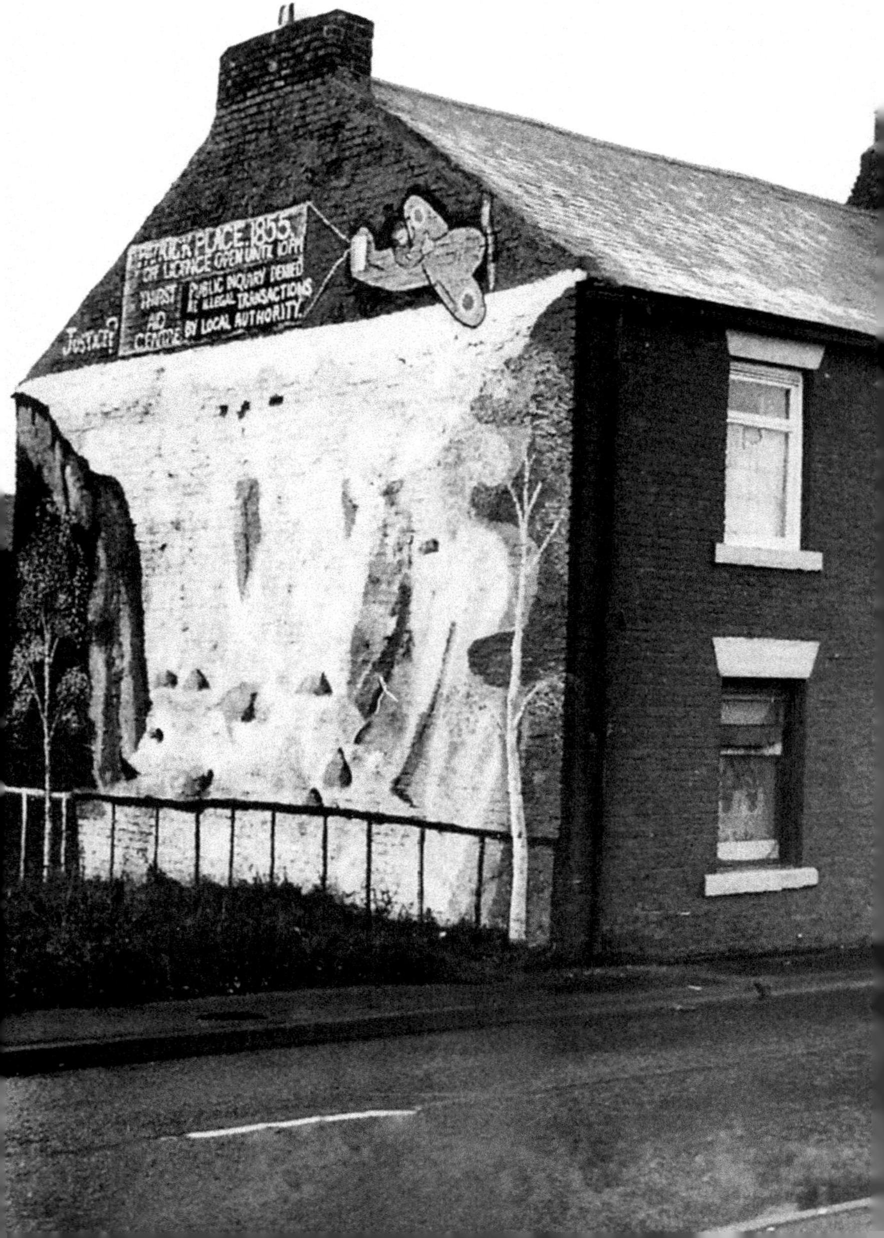
PLACE 1855
OFF LICENCE OPEN UNTIL 10PM
THIRST AID CENTRE
PUBLIC INQUIRY DENIED RE ILLEGAL TRANSACTIONS BY LOCAL AUTHORITY.
JUSTICE?

39. PATRICK'S PLACE, WAGONWAY ROAD, *c.* 1980

Patrick's shop wall mural brightened up drab Wagonway Road for years. Patrick's, a long established grocery and off-licence business, doggedly protested against compulsory purchase until finally succumbing to demolition in the 1990s. Occasionally still referred to as 'the low road', Wagonway Road lies close to the route once taken by coal trucks from 'C' pit to the riverside staiths. What is now a well-maintained carriageway was condemned in 1885 as the most 'crying evil in the district'.

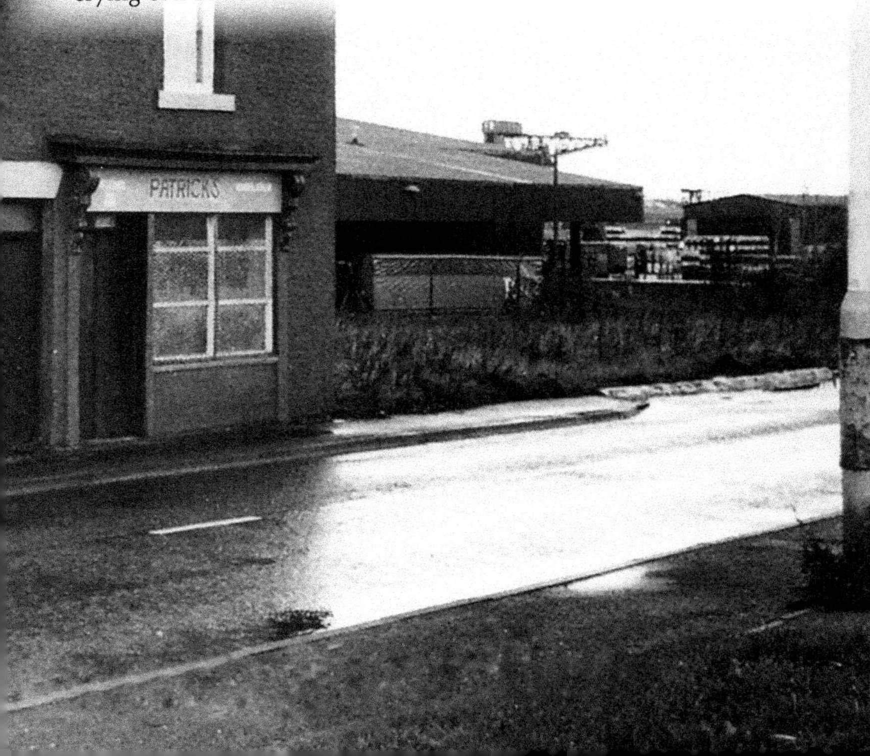

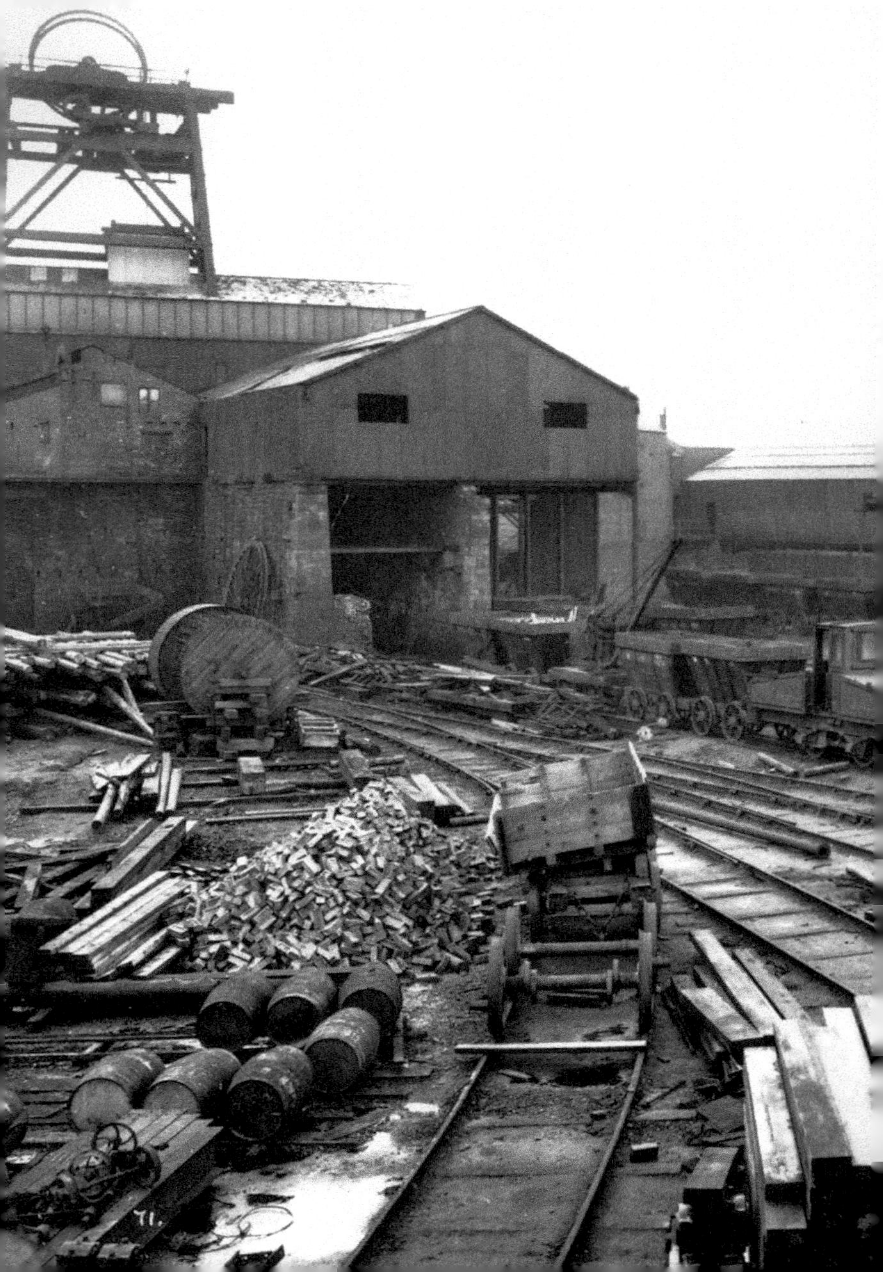

40. HEBBURN COLLIERY 'A' PIT, 1922

At more than 700 feet, 'A' pit was Hebburn's first deep coal mine. Heavy flooding was encountered during its sinking in the 1790s and gas remained a constant danger – explosions in 1805 and 1849 killed a total of sixty-nine men and boys. By 1900, around 1,300 colliers were employed but in 1931 the financial collapse of the Wallsend & Hebburn Coal Company effectively ended mining in Hebburn. 'A' pit is now covered by the 1990s Walsh Avenue estate.

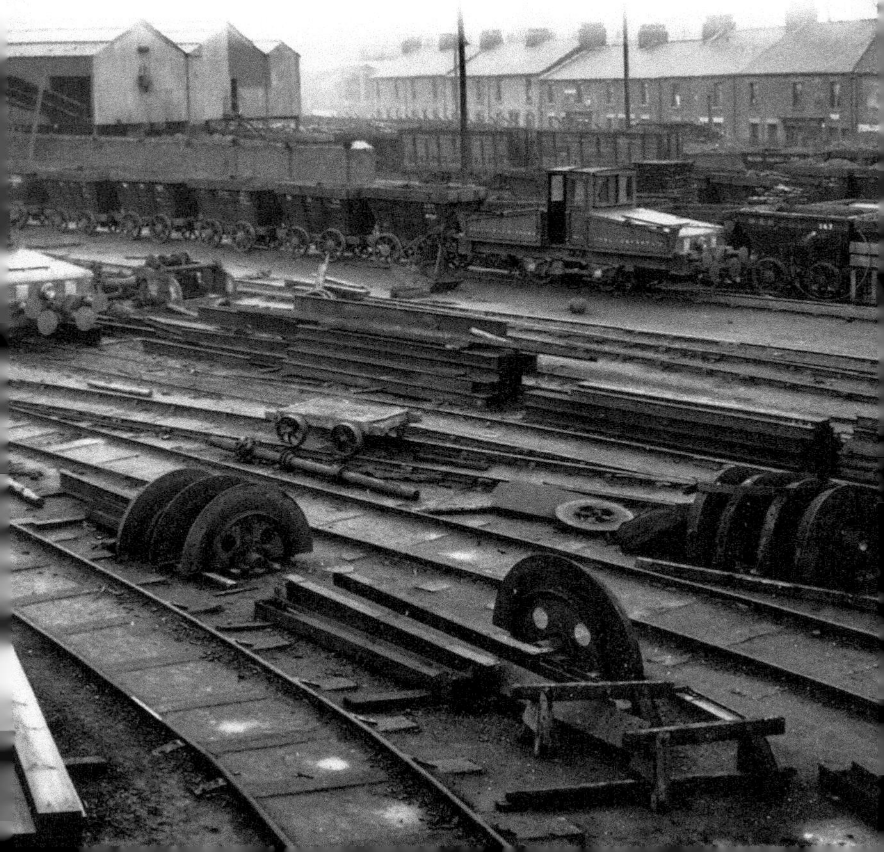

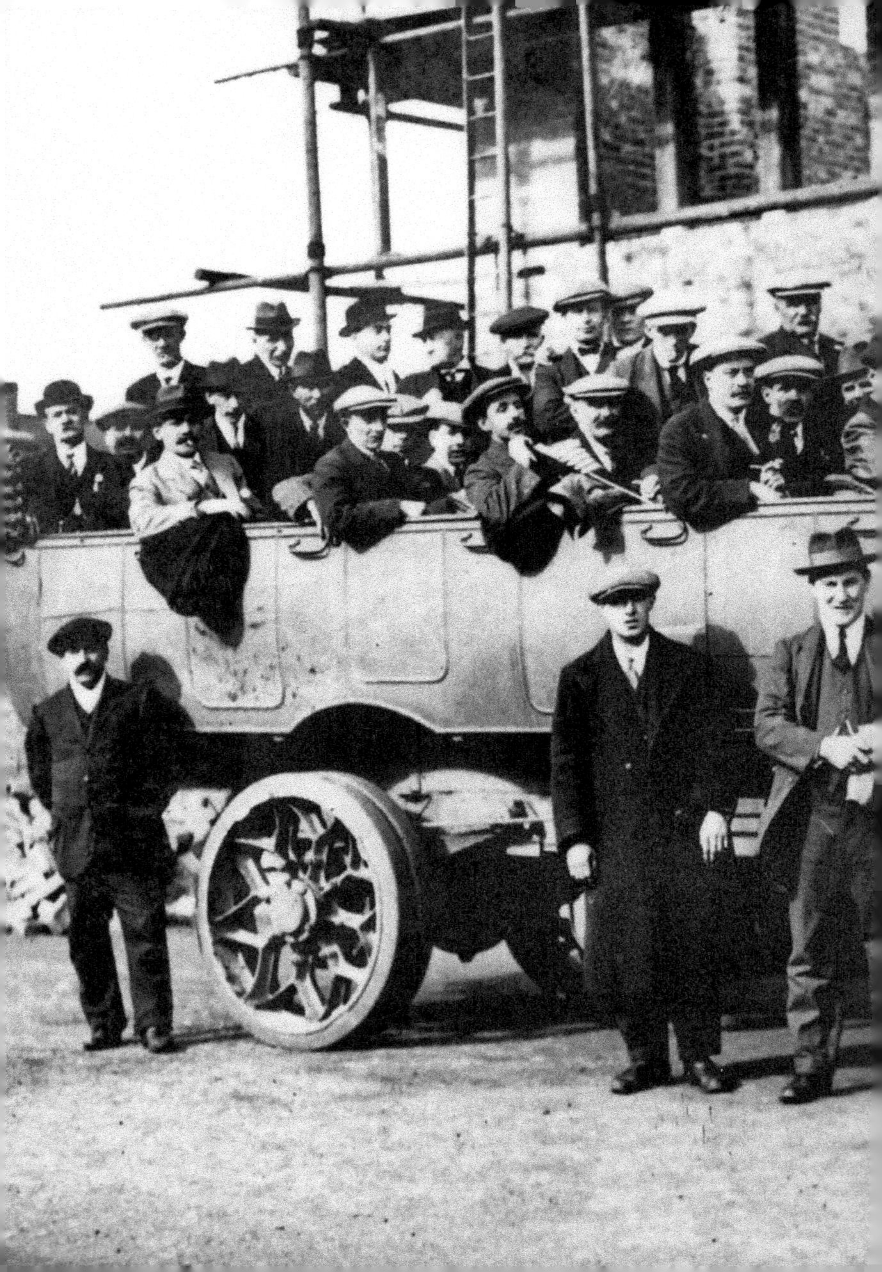

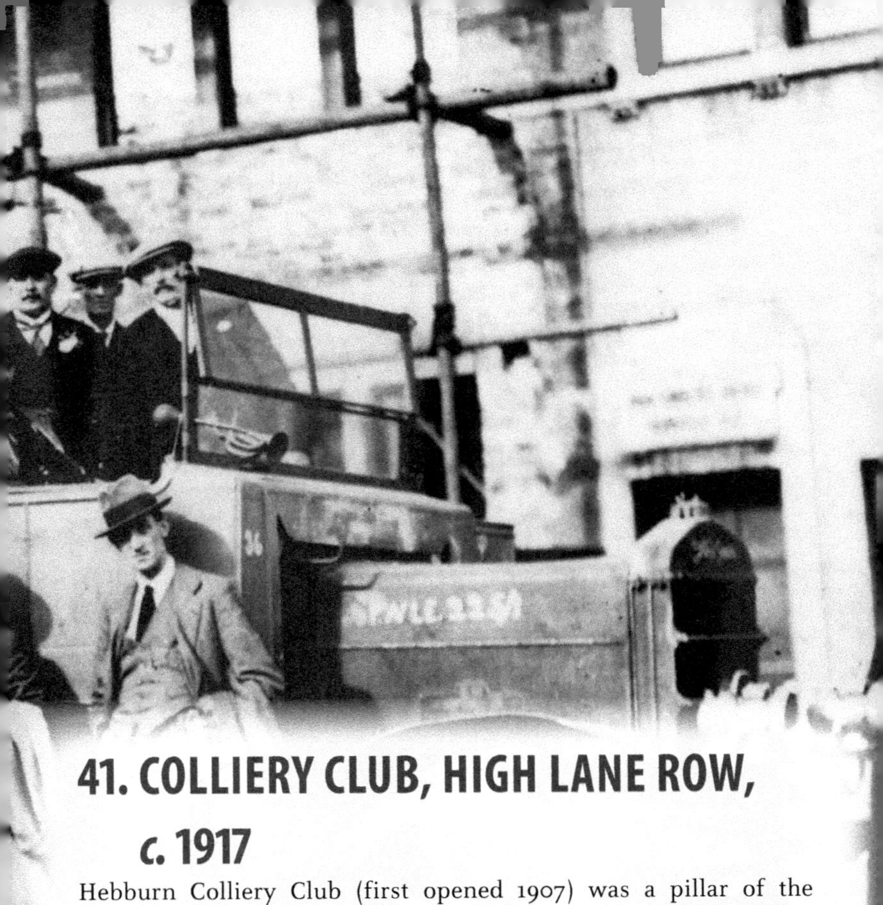

41. COLLIERY CLUB, HIGH LANE ROW, *c.* 1917

Hebburn Colliery Club (first opened 1907) was a pillar of the mining community – a venue for meetings and games as well as drinking. Working men's clubs and institutes began to appear in the late nineteenth century, but were not licensed to sell alcohol until 1902. Among bus trippers outside the club – which is under reconstruction after a fire – is colliery weighman John Coltman (flower in lapel) whose job helped to determine the pitmen's wages. A new club was built nearby in 1971.

42. HIGH LANE HOTEL, *c.* 1970

Simpson's Hotel dominated the east side of High Lane Row. Originally built for Palmer's workmen, the big, barrack-style block was opened in 1919, then taken over by the Simpson Hotel Company and associated with the Simpson name. Simpson's was called a hostel but was advertised as an 'industrial hotel' and in 1975 lodged 200 men. High modernisation costs shut its doors. By 1998 it had been completely demolished to make way for a new estate, which includes Coppergate House, a small hostel for the homeless.

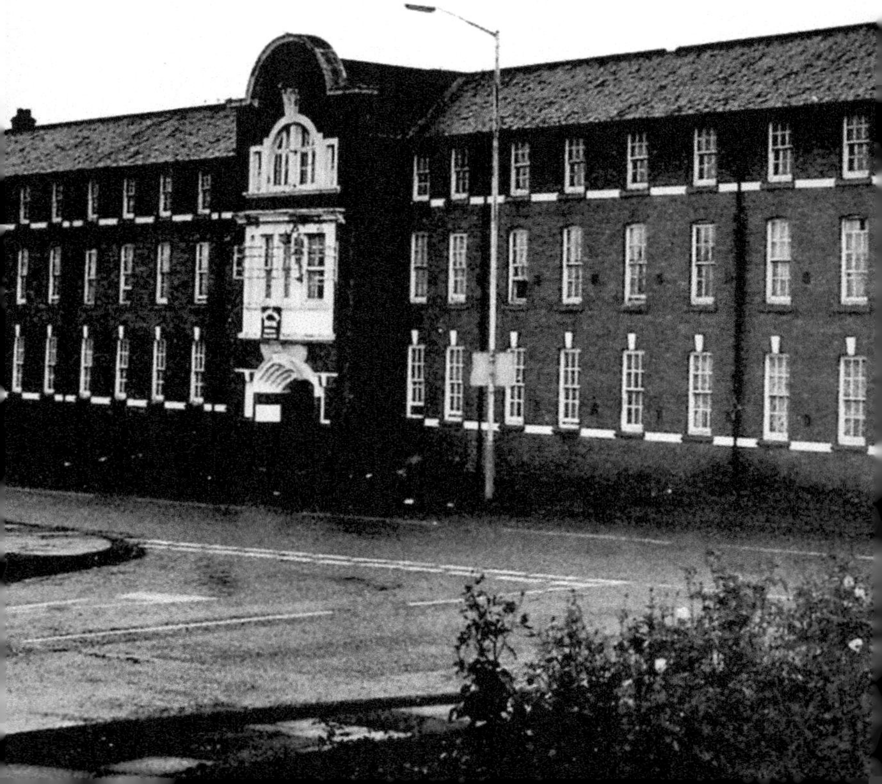

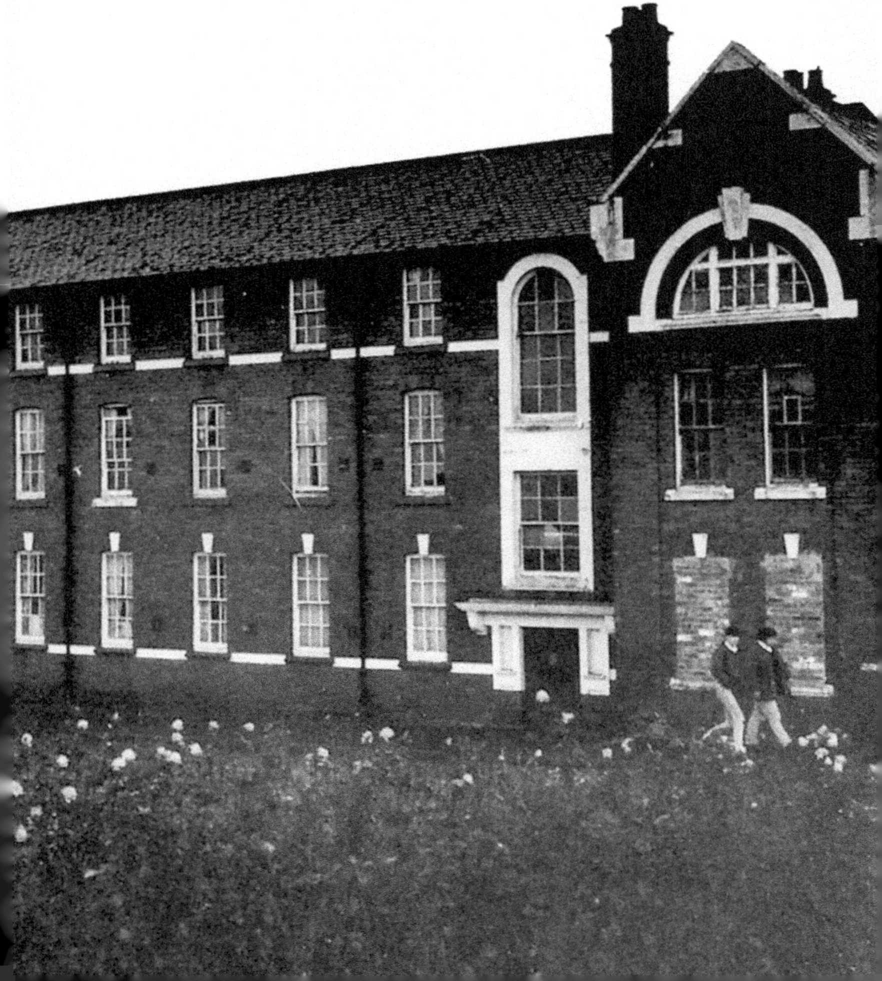

43. CHAPEL ROW BACK LANE, HEBBURN COLLIERY 'A' PIT, *c.* 1900

Chapel Row was part of an area called The Square, built near the pithead. The row's dozen houses appear to have been better than the average pit village accommodation. Although lacking ventilation, their two rooms were thought to be acceptable by Durham's medical officer. However, his 1888 report goes on to condemn adjacent rented property as 'grossly insanitary'. That could never be said of the neat properties of Brancepeth and Auckland Roads, which now sit comfortably on this historic site.

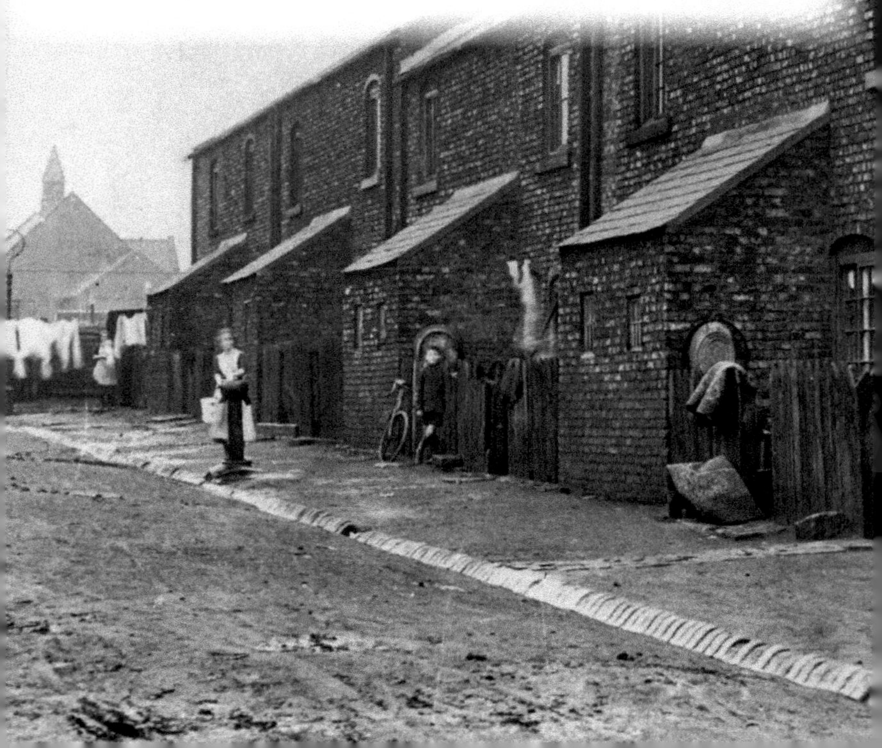

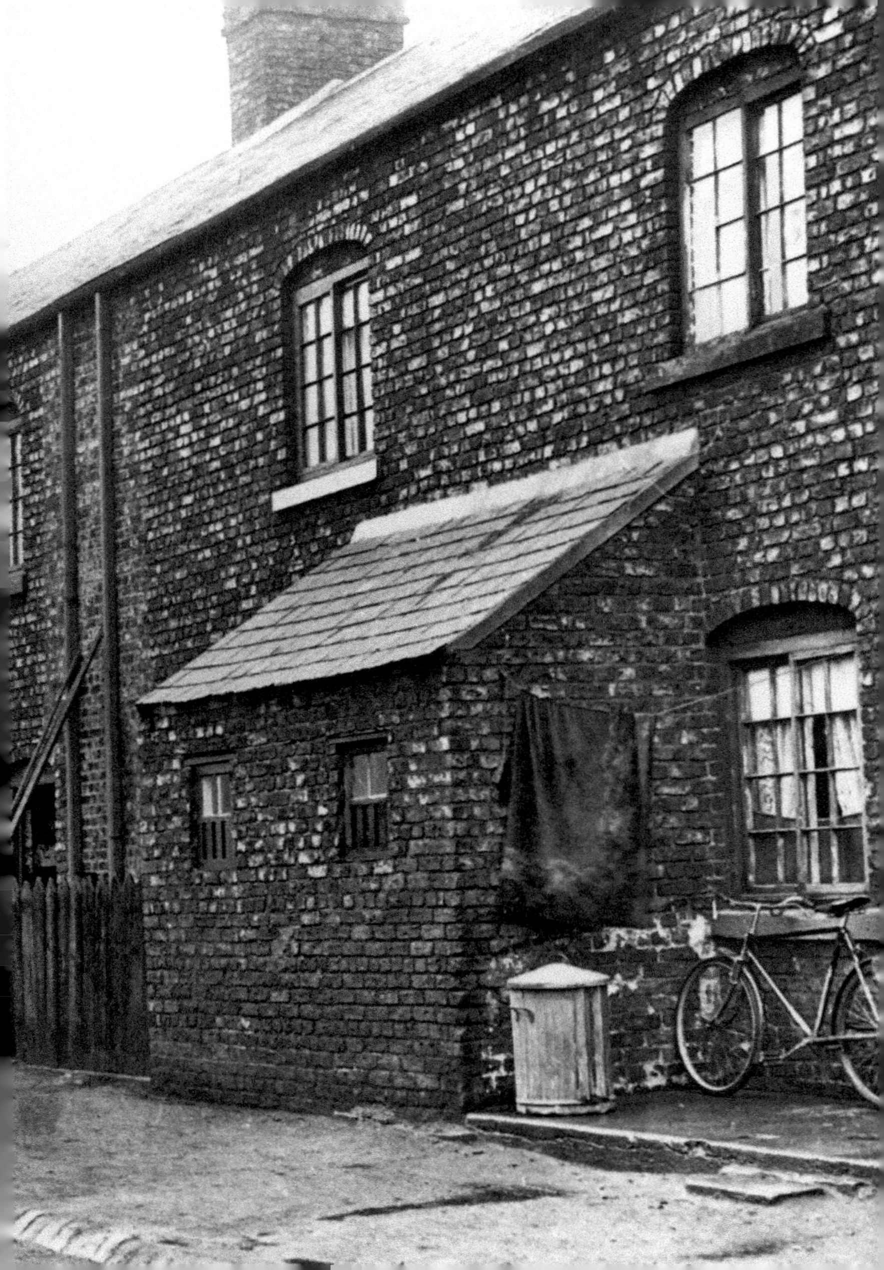

44. BEDE'S WELL, 1932

St Bede's Well is shown here after a publicly funded restoration in the late 1920s. The railed enclosure was erected as protection not just from inquisitive schoolboys, but also from the dumping of slag that was in full swing at that time. Although historical proof is lacking, this former old watercourse in a small valley of the Bede Burn is traditionally associated with the famed local saint. It was given a new look in the 1980s.

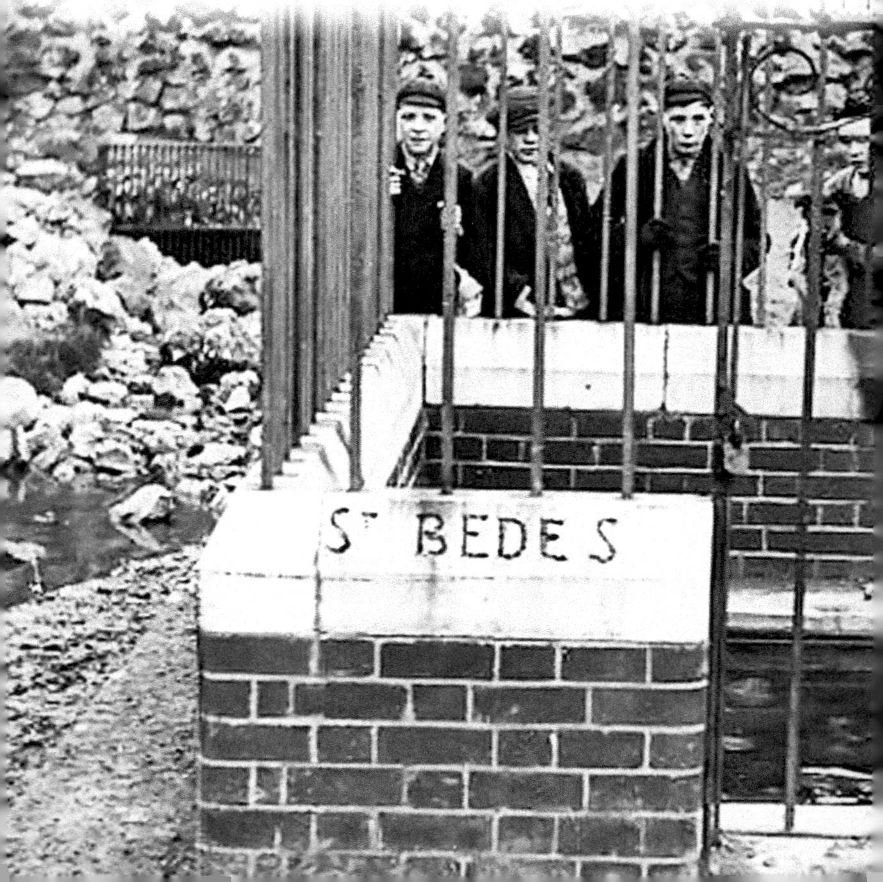

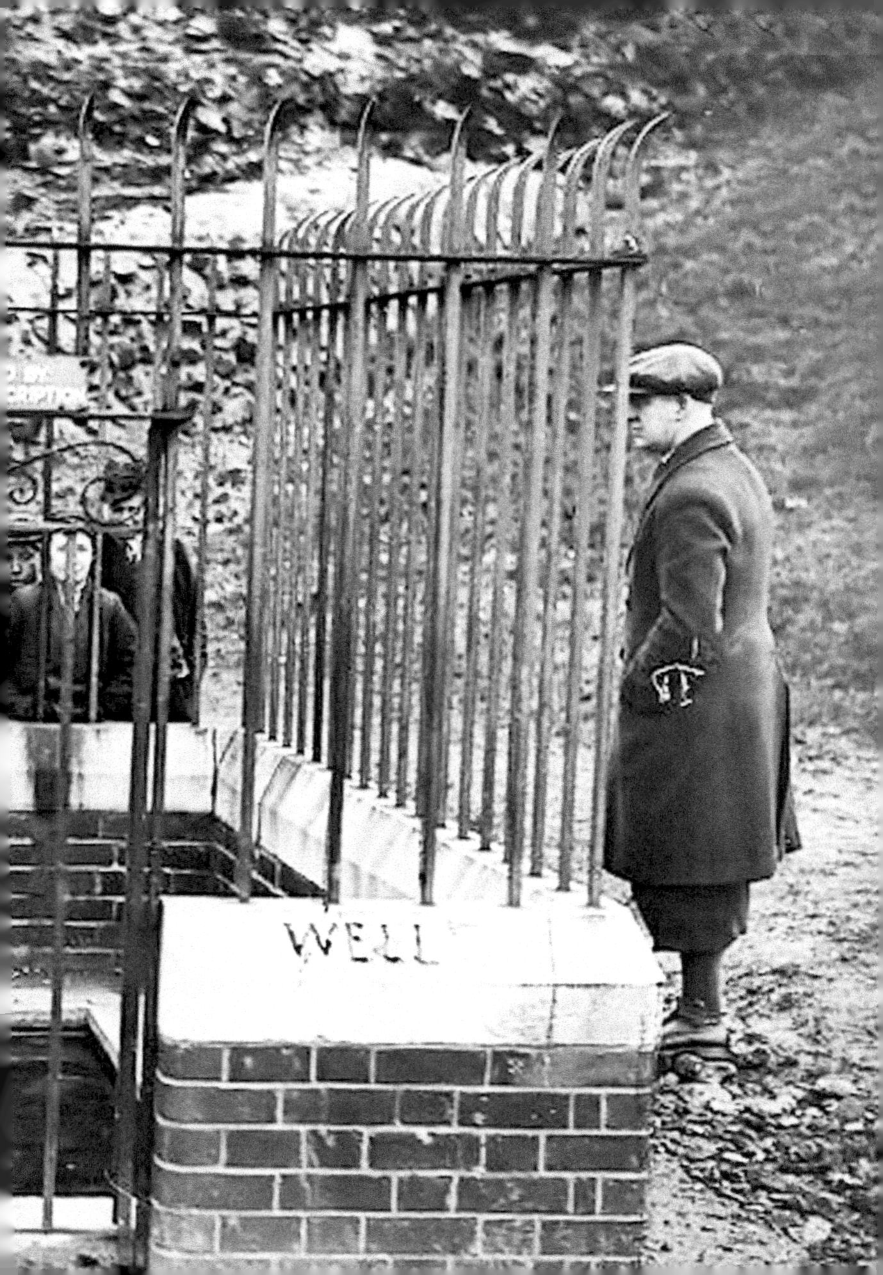
WELL

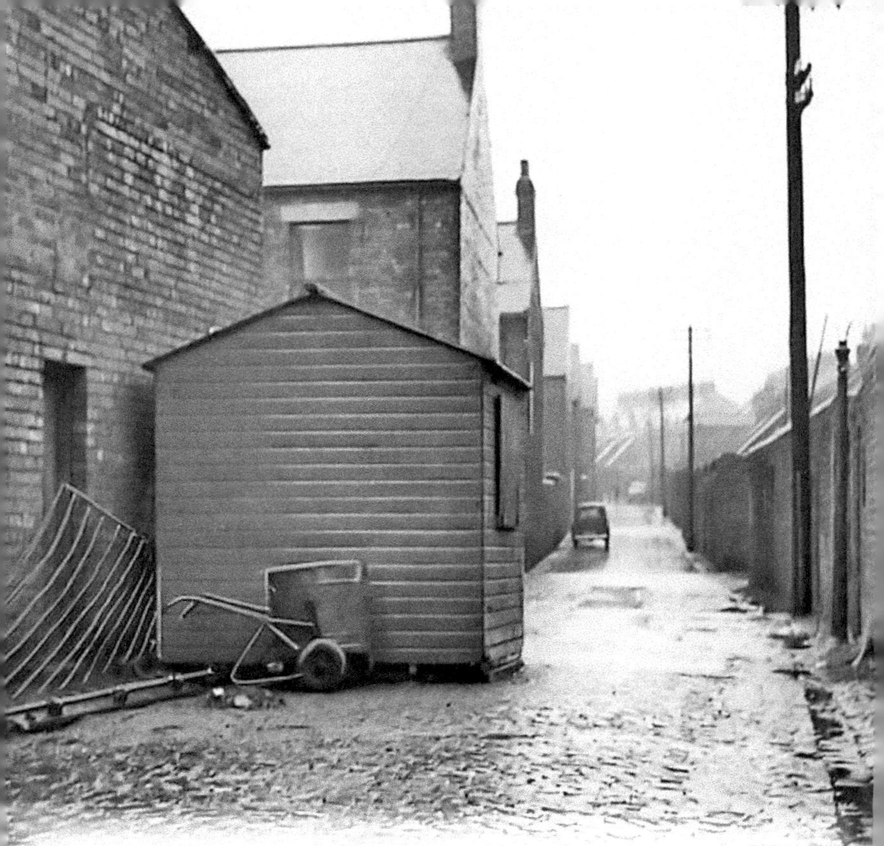

45. VICTORIA ROAD EAST, BACK LANE, *c.* 1962

This atmospheric photograph captures a typical Tyneside scene. Rain-soaked cobbles behind Victoria Road stretch past the gable ends of Northborne Road, Collingwood, Howe and Frobisher Streets. Half a century on, many of the old terraced houses remain. Fitted with modern kitchen and bathroom extensions, they have outlasted several much newer housing developments in Hebburn.